THE FABULOUS DECADE

Alan S. Blinder and Janet L. Yellen

THE FABULOUS DECADE

Macroeconomic Lessons from the 1990s

A Century Foundation Report

The Century Foundation Press • New York

The Century Foundation sponsors and supervises timely analyses of economic policy, foreign affairs, and domestic political issues. Not-for-profit and nonpartisan, it was founded in 1919 and endowed by Edward A. Filene.

LIBRARY OF CONGRESS CATALOGING-IN-PUBLICATION DATA
Blinder, Alan S.
  The fabulous decade : macroeconomic lessons from the 1990s / by Alan S. Blinder and Janet L. Yellen.
    p. cm.
  Includes bibliographical references and index.
  ISBN 0-87078-467-6 (pbk. : alk. paper)
    1. United States—Economic policy—1993–   . 2. United States—Fiscal policy. 3. United States—Monetary policy. 4. United States—Economic conditions—1981–   . I. Yellen, Janet L. (Janet Louise), 1946–   . II. Title.
  HC106.82 .B584 2001
  330.973'0928—dc21

                                                              2001003089

Cover design and photo montage by Claude Goodwin
Manufactured in the United States of America.

FOREWORD

Perhaps the best way to appreciate how robust economic conditions were during the latter half of the 1990s is to recall just how much time was devoted to analyzing what the end would be like. The numerous accounts predicting "soft or hard landings" when the boom times faded had a common quality: they all seemed to reflect an underlying belief that the prosperity we were experiencing was just too good to be true. Some called it the Goldilocks economy—not too hot and not too cold, but just right. Democrats credited the policies of the Clinton administration, and some Republicans tried to explain that it was all merely a delayed reaction to the policies of President Reagan during the 1980s. There may be no simple right answer to the question of why conditions were so good, but one judgment that warrants little dispute is that, somehow, a combination of policy and good fortune produced better economic circumstances for most Americans.

Indeed, for the foreseeable future, the prosperity that the United States enjoyed during the last five years of the 1990s is likely to be the gold standard in terms of economic performance. Growth rates averaged 4.0 percent over that span; productivity increases, which averaged only 1.4 percent from 1973 to 1990, averaged almost twice that in the second half of the 1990s; unemployment declined from 7.8 percent in 1992 to 4.1 percent by the end of the decade; and inflation, contrary to prevailing attitudes among economists about what was possible under such boom conditions, averaged only 2.9 percent for the period. Of course, the greatest attention was paid to perhaps the least useful of these statistics, the increase of the Dow from under 3,000 in 1990 to a high of over 11,700 in 2000.

Among professional economists, the meaning of these statistics is likely to provoke lively debates for many years to come. The economy's performance not only represented a discontinuity with that of the previous two decades but also justified the beliefs of the skeptical minority among analysts who argued that high employment, rapid growth, and low inflation were, in fact, compatible.

Impressed by the many questions raised by the performance of the economy during the 1990s, The Century Foundation and the Russell Sage Foundation formed a joint venture designed to discover what economic lessons could be learned from the decade, particularly in terms of the unpredicted low levels of both unemployment and inflation and the high levels of growth. We were very fortunate to secure Robert Solow, a Nobel Laureate in Economics and Professor Emeritus at the Massachusetts Institute of Technology, and Alan Krueger, Bendheim Professor of Economics and Public Affairs at Princeton University and editor of *The Journal of Economic Perspectives*, to serve as cochairs of the working group that was formed to conduct this analysis. Solow and Krueger assembled an extraordinary group of economists to join in the exploration and to develop a set of topics for individual papers that would explore the conditions, and especially the policies—in labor markets and the broader economy—that enabled the economic performance of the 1990s. These papers will be published later this year in a single volume. In addition, Robert Solow is planning to write a book summarizing the findings of the group for a broader audience.

As part of the overall effort, two members of the working group—both distinguished economists who played key government roles in shaping the economic policies of the 1990s—agreed to recount their unique insiders' view of the economic trends and policies that gave us the "golden decade." Alan Blinder, professor of economics at Princeton University, served on the Council of Economic Advisers in the first Clinton administration and then as vice chairman of the Board of Governors of the Federal Reserve system from 1994 to early 1996. Janet Yellen, professor of business and economics at the University of California at Berkeley, was a member of the Federal Reserve Board from 1994 to 1997 and then served as chair of the Council of Economic Advisers at the end of the second Clinton administration. In the pages that follow, with insight and candor, the authors deal with every major component of fiscal and monetary policy, politics, and happenstance that might have played a role in determining the overall economic performance of the 1990s. It is an important story, with potentially significant implications for the future of American economic studies and policies.

To help us understand what happened, the authors remind us of the consequences of the huge tax cuts and unprecedented peacetime deficits of the 1980s. Somewhat oddly under the rhetorically anti-government Reagan administration, these actions amounted to an enormous public sector intervention in the economy. They created extraordinary fiscal conditions that came hard on the heels of some of the sternest monetary policies in the nation's history—policies justified as necessary strong medicine to cure the energy and commodity-driven inflation of the late 1970s.

There followed a significant policy shift in the 1990s, when both Presidents Bush and Clinton signed important tax increases. Subsequently, the Clinton administration was successful in forging a series of budgets that helped to bring about the dramatic turn from large deficits to large surpluses. The enormity of the revisions in the Congressional Budget Office forecasts over this period reveal how huge the transformation was. In 1997, for example, the CBO projected a fiscal year 2001 deficit of $167 billion; three years later the same agency predicted a surplus of $235 billion for the same year. (One might imagine that such swings would restrain those who plan enormous tax cuts or expenditure programs premised on projections ten or even more years in advance.) Almost incredibly, some analysts began to speculate about the impact of paying off the federal debt, leaving no Treasury securities at all in the hands of the public.

In all this, the possibility that plain luck played a role was substantial enough to make it a part of every comprehensive conversation about what made the 1990s so golden. Blinder and Yellen explore that aspect of the story in detail. The danger is that some will make too much of fortunate circumstances. The policy decisions made during the 1990s had far-reaching consequences for both growth and low inflation. And, of course, the real lessons for the future lie in the study of what was done right, not in remembering to keep our fingers crossed. It also is important to keep in mind that the choices made by national leaders were not easy. Taxes were raised and spending limited, reassuring the financial and business sectors, as well as foreign investors, that the nation's fiscal policy had changed fundamentally since the era of big deficits. With regard to monetary policy, the Federal Reserve showed surprising willingness to sustain considerably higher levels of growth than had been anticipated. In this, the central bank demonstrated unusual flexibility, staying the expansionary course even after unemployment fell from 6, to 5, and then to 4 percent.

Overall, perhaps the most interesting thing about the 1990s is that the conventional wisdom about what could be achieved in terms of economic performance turned out to be unnecessarily pessimistic. This lesson has enormous implications for how we ought to conceive and judge policy in the future. Given the possibility of more rapid growth, tolerating slower growth requires justification. If we can learn to sustain 1990s-style prosperity at levels that are by no means unprecedented, we will be able to solve a great many of the most pressing problems facing our nation. We can fund Social Security and Medicare, for example—and still meet the need for better schools and improved infrastructure. None of this is to say that we have found a way to repeal the business cycle—there will surely be down periods as well as good times—or that we do not need whatever breaks fortune will bring our way. But, to perhaps a greater extent than we thought, we can still be the captain of our ship. We can choose wisely or badly. That is what Blinder and Yellen help us understand in this important work.

RICHARD C. LEONE, *President*
The Century Foundation
May 2001

ERIC WANNER, *President*
Russell Sage Foundation
May 2001

CONTENTS

ACKNOWLEDGMENTS

The authors are deeply indebted to David Reifschneider, Chris Varvares, and Joel Prakken for conducting the simulations reported in this paper; to George Akerlof, Steven Braun, Alan Krueger, Alicia Munnell, and Robert Solow for helpful comments; and to Celina Su, Meghan McNally, and Ryan Edwards for able research assistance. Yellen is grateful to the Russell Sage Foundation for financial support.

1.

INTRODUCTION

Macroeconomically speaking, the 1990s, and especially the second half of the decade, were a remarkably successful period for the United States. (See Table 1.1, page 2.) Early in the decade, no one would have bet that the 1990s would prove to be the most fabulous decade since the 1960s. Inflation had flared up in 1989–90, the economy suffered a recession in 1990–91, and Americans told pollsters at the time of the 1992 election that they were quite pessimistic about the economic outlook. But all that was to change dramatically in the ensuing years.

The unemployment rate, which reached a decade high of 7.8 percent in June 1992, fell steadily thereafter and ended the 1990s at 4.1 percent—the lowest level since the late 1960s. Despite this extraordinary employment performance, the inflation rate (measured by the twelve-month trailing consumer price index [CPI]), which hit a decade high of 6.3 percent in October and November 1990, declined to 2.7 percent by December 1999. By the decade's end, there was even a developing consensus that America's productivity growth rate, which had languished near 1.4 percent for more than twenty years, was perking up—perhaps substantially.[1]

How and why did all these wonderful things happen to the U.S. economy? What constellation of good policies, good luck, and related historical developments provided the underpinnings for all this good news? And can we expect it to last? Most important, what lessons should we take away from this period? These are the questions to be explored in the pages that follow.

1

TABLE 1.1. ECONOMIC PERFORMANCE BY DECADE

	1990s	(SECOND HALF)	1980s	1970s	1960s
Real GDP growth (%)[a]	3.2	(4.0)	3.0	3.3	4.4
Unemployment rate (%)[b]	5.8	(5.0)	7.3	6.2	4.8
Inflation rate (%)[c]	2.9	(2.4)	5.1	7.4	2.5

[a] Average compound growth rate from last quarter of previous decade to last quarter of stated decade, seasonally adjusted at annual rates.
[b] Average civilian unemployment rate for the 120 months of each decade.
[c] Average compound rate of increase of the consumer price index from December of the previous decade to December of the stated decade, annualized.

Source: GDP growth figures are from the U.S. Department of Commerce, Bureau of Economic Analysis; unemployment rate and inflation rate are from the U.S. Department of Labor, Bureau of Labor Statistics.

2.

THE SETTING

The calendar does not always align with historical events. In terms of economic history, the marvelous "Sixties" probably began around 1962 and ended around 1973. Similarly, the unhappy "Seventies" probably stretched from late 1973 until 1983 or so. True to form, in terms of macroeconomic events, the "Nineties" can be said to have started in 1992 or 1993 and now look like they may have ended in 2000. (But, at this writing, it is too early to tell for sure.)

During the 1992 presidential campaign, no one could have imagined what a wonderful position the U.S. economy would be in by the end of the decade. Then-Governor Bill Clinton's famous campaign motto, "It's the economy, stupid," graphically pointed out the terrific political opportunity—for the challenger—that had been created by the widespread voter discontent with the state of the economy. Consider:

- The recovery from the 1990–91 recession was both weak by historical standards and remarkably "jobless" in its early stages. Nonfarm payroll employment rose by just 611,000 jobs between the March 1991 recession trough and October 1992, a mere 36,000 per month (compared with the 250,000 or so monthly gains that would become the norm later). Furthermore, more than half of these meager employment gains were in government jobs. Not only were payrolls barely expanding, but many employed Americans plainly were worried about retaining their jobs.

- Real wages had been doing miserably for years. Misleading but widely cited numbers suggested at the time (and after) that the

3

average real wage had not advanced in over twenty-five years.[1] While that was certainly incorrect, the truth was bad enough: productivity and real wages had stagnated since about 1973. And during the decade ending in 1992, real wages failed to keep up with even the sluggish growth of labor productivity.[2]

- Median real wages had done even worse than mean real wages, because wage inequality had been rising since around 1980.[3] Thus the "typical" worker had done worse than the average numbers suggested.

- The large and growing federal budget deficit was the source of a great deal of angst—not only in financial circles, where the "bond market vigilantes" were in high dudgeon, but also among the general public. It came to be seen as a symbol of government incompetence.

In fact, the U.S. economy was not in nearly as bad shape as the citizenry thought at the time. Economic growth during the four quarters of 1992 averaged a hefty 4 percent. Inflation, which had briefly spiked above 6 percent in 1989 and 1990, had been pushed back down to about 3 percent. But all this was little solace to incumbent President George Bush as Bill Clinton hammered away on the economic issue. It was voter perceptions that mattered. A *Wall Street Journal*/NBC News poll as late as mid-September found that an astonishing 86 percent of Americans believed the country was still in a recession. That was a full eighteen months after the recession trough. Fully two-thirds thought the country was "on the wrong track," whatever that means.[4] Just a few days before the election, *USA Today* reported that 60 percent of voters thought economic conditions were getting worse, while only 28 percent believed they were improving.[5] The public was wrong; the economy was definitely on the mend. But this misconception surely hurt President Bush at the polls. Such lags of public perceptions behind economic realities are not unusual; in this case, they may have been helped along by the fact that job growth was unusually weak early in the recovery.

More important for our story, three of the foundation stones for what was to become the Fabulous Decade had already been put in place: tighter fiscal policy, looser monetary policy, and industrial restructuring that made American business "leaner and meaner." We begin the story with fiscal policy.

① THE BUDGET AGREEMENT OF 1990

The 1990 budget agreement was much maligned at the time, and proved to be a political albatross around the neck of President Bush. As a candidate in 1988, he had famously pledged "no new taxes." But as president in 1990, he acceded to Democratic demands for higher taxes to reduce the deficit. Despite its bad press, the agreement marked the first giant step down a path that would eventually lead the federal government to sizable budget surpluses. Unfortunately, contemporary observers did not see it that way. What they saw, instead, was that the budget deficit was on the rise despite the so-called deficit reduction package. That made the 1990 budget agreement look bad, and it was prematurely and unfairly pronounced a failure.

In fact, the two main reasons why the budget deficit rose rather than fell after 1990 were not failures of the agreement at all. Instead, they were (1) the 1990–91 recession, which raised the annual deficits by about $160 billion between fiscal years 1991 and 1993 (according to Congressional Budget Office [CBO] estimates), and (2) the huge costs of mopping up after the savings and loan debacle—which averaged over $60 billion a year in fiscal years 1990 and 1991. But never mind. The seemingly inexorable rise of the deficit, coupled with the remnants of Reaganite hostility to tax hikes, conspired to give the 1990 agreement a bad name.

The budget agreement also included a real sleeper: the Budget Enforcement Act (BEA) of 1990. This seemingly boring procedural innovation was barely noticed at the time, but it would assume great importance in the coming years. Prior to 1990, Congress had tried to use the Gramm-Rudman-Hollings (GRH) approach to tie itself to the mast of deficit reduction. Under GRH, a five-year program that was first enacted in 1985 and then modified (after failing) in 1987, Congress set legally binding targets for each year's budget deficit. If Congress failed to enact legislation to comply with that year's deficit target, an automatic "sequester" was supposed to enforce the target via equiproportionate reductions in most categories of spending.

The central problem with GRH was clear to economists at the outset and eventually became clear to members of Congress as well: the law set a target for an endogenous variable that Congress cannot control—the budget deficit. What Congress can and does control are (1) tax rates and other provisions of the tax code, (2) the rules governing the generosity of and eligibility for entitlement programs, and

(3) the volume of discretionary spending on the programs that receive annual appropriations (which constitute a minority of the budget). Wisely, these were precisely the three items on which the Budget Enforcement Act focused congressional attention.

Discretionary spending was limited by annual "caps," much as in the GRH approach—but with an important difference: the caps applied to something Congress actually could control. Taxes and entitlements were grouped together in a separate pay-as-you-go, or "PAYGO," pool. Under the BEA rules, any member of Congress who proposed a tax cut or an increase in entitlement spending was obligated to propose offsetting revenue increases or cuts in other entitlements to "pay for" it. In other words, within the portion of the budget covered by the PAYGO requirement—the clear majority—the new rule was budget balance *at the margin.* But endogenous changes in the budget due to, say, changes in the economy were not to elicit any policy response.

The new approach worked. Unlike GRH, under which Congress repeatedly changed its deficit targets but violated them anyway, the BEA established rules by which Congress could and did live. Indeed, the enforcement mechanisms established in 1990 played pivotal roles in keeping spending in check in several subsequent budget battles. Furthermore, they endured and remain on the books through fiscal year 2002.

② BUSINESS RESTRUCTURING

Industrial restructuring was probably even more important than the 1990 budget agreement.[6] By 1992, the nation had already proceeded pretty far down the difficult path that was popularly (though somewhat misleadingly) referred to as "downsizing"—something it accomplished well ahead of the rest of the world.[7] Why did restructuring come first to, and go furthest in, America? That is an issue that merits thorough exploration—but not in this book. We will just briefly mention two reasons. One is that the United States has always practiced a more hard-edged brand of capitalism than either Europe or Japan. Legal barriers to layoffs are negligible in this country, and the government does not make them difficult by regulatory means. There is not even much social disapprobation. The European and Japanese traditions, though changing of late, are starkly different in all these respects.

The second reason is the behavior of the exchange rate, which rarely receives even a mention in this context. The pruning of American industry began in the severe recession of 1981–83, but it gained further momentum in the mid-1980s under the pressure of a grotesquely overvalued dollar. The super-dollar rendered U.S.-made products uncompetitive in world markets, thereby showing American firms the hangman's noose. Just as Dr. Johnson had anticipated, that concentrated their minds. In the ensuing struggle to survive, the fittest reduced slack, slimmed down, and became more efficient. The weaker firms perished. Both developments increased the efficiency of U.S. businesses, especially in the heavily exposed manufacturing sector.

The U.S. financial system was also brusquely restructured at the time. The bad loan problems that had decimated the savings and loan industry spread to the commercial banks (who added a few mistakes of their own) in the 1980s, and bank failures rose to levels not seen in America since the advent of federal deposit insurance. The banking system was thus in a vulnerable position when the recession of 1990–91 hit it with a further body blow, leaving our financial system in its weakest condition in decades. This financial fragility, in turn, created some of the major "headwinds" that were cited at the time as serious impediments to recovery. (More on this in Chapter 3.)

The difficult period of industrial and financial restructuring certainly had its dark side: job losses were rampant and American workers felt insecure and powerless. But our harsh brand of industrial Darwinism probably left American businesses "leaner and meaner" in the end. As we will discuss in Chapter 6, it may also have left the U.S. economy with a more favorable Phillips curve, as traumatized workers pushed less aggressively for wage increases.

Starting around 1992 or 1993, and helped by the lagged effects of a cheaper dollar, American businesses began to reap the rewards for their earlier investments in restructuring. The process began to move into a new phase that placed more emphasis on "leaner" and less on "meaner." As this process progressed, the harsh climate that labor faced as late as 1992 began to give way to a new, more productive industrial environment in which capitalists enjoyed higher profits and workers enjoyed greater employment. With economic activity picking up, American businesses were well positioned to capitalize on the new opportunities.

One simple numerical indication of this transition comes from the American Management Association's annual survey of downsizing.

Each year, the AMA asks its members whether they eliminated jobs (both gross and net) in the previous year and, if so, how many. Table 2.1 shows a sample of the results.[8] Multiplying the fraction of firms reporting net job elimination (column 1) by the average percentage job reduction among such firms (column 2) produces a handy summary measure of the extent of downsizing in the American job market as a whole (column 3). Clearly, the picture for labor improved markedly between the 1992–93 and 1994–95 surveys. The typical firm in the survey—which is, unfortunately, not a random sample of all U.S. firms—shed almost 4.5 percent of its labor annually in the three-year period from mid-1990 to mid-1993, but only about 2.5 percent in the three years from mid-1994 to mid-1997.

TABLE 2.1. AMERICAN MANAGEMENT
ASSOCIATION DOWNSIZING SURVEYS

TWELVE MONTHS ENDING	(1) PERCENTAGE REPORTING ELIMINATING JOBS	(2) AVERAGE PERCENTAGE REDUCTION AMONG THESE	(3) (1) x (2)
June 1991	43.8	11.4	5.0
June 1992	36.0	10.5	3.8
June 1993	32.6	13.9	4.5
June 1994	30.3	NA	—
June 1995	27.3	10.2	2.8
June 1996	27.9	10.4	2.9
June 1997	19.0	10.7	2.0

Source: American Management Association, private communication.

The data from the government's Displaced Workers Survey, which *are* a random sample (but of workers, not of businesses), tell a similar story but with somewhat different timing. Tabulations of these data, summarized in Table 2.2, show a notable drop-off in the rate of job displacement between the 1993–95 period and 1995–97.[9] (Since these are three-year displacement rates, the year 1995 belongs to both periods.) In either case, our basic point is the same: the jobs famine of early 1990s helped set the stage for the feast that was to come.

TABLE 2.2. DISPLACED WORKER SURVEYS

THREE-YEAR PERIOD	RATE OF JOB LOSS (%)
1989–91	11.8
1991–93	10.9
1993–95	11.5
1995–97	9.1
1997–99	8.6

Source: Henry S. Farber, "Job Loss in the United States, 1981–1999," Working Paper #452, Industrial Relations Section, Princeton University, April 2001.

③ MONETARY POLICY

The Federal Reserve was severely criticized in 1991 and 1992 for not providing more support to what was, at first, a very weak recovery from recession. Indeed, President George Bush blamed Federal Reserve Chairman Alan Greenspan for costing him the election—which may well have been true. But the Fed finally brought the federal funds rate down to about 3 percent—roughly equal to the rate of inflation—by the middle of 1992. That was too late for George Bush, but not too late to contribute to the subsequent economic expansion. Most important for our story, the Fed then held the real federal funds rate at about zero for over eighteen months—thereby providing a hefty and sustained dose of monetary stimulus.

Thus, as President Bill Clinton took the oath of office in January 1993, three key ingredients for macroeconomic success were at least partly in place:

- Although it was not recognized at the time, the alarming path toward ever-rising federal budget deficits (as a share of gross domestic product [GDP]) had been deflected downward by the 1990 budget agreement.

- Many U.S. businesses had slimmed down and become more efficient. In addition, the dollar had tumbled from its 1985 highs. Both of these factors made American industry once again competitive on world markets.

- The Fed had lowered the real federal funds rate to zero and had its foot pressed firmly on the monetary accelerator.

Notice the beginnings here of what were to become the two major themes of the 1990s: a shift in the policy mix toward tighter budgets and easier monetary policy, and improvements in the efficiency of American industry. However, the pre-1993 developments only set the stage. Decisive monetary and fiscal actions were required to unleash the potential, and productivity was as yet showing no signs of accelerating. (In fact, productivity performance was weak during the first half of the 1990s.) What made the Fabulous Decade so fabulous is that all this did happen in the ensuing years.

3.

LAGS AND THE FED'S SUSTAINED EASY-MONEY POLICY

As just mentioned, the Federal Reserve was accused of being insufficiently aggressive in cutting interest rates during and after the 1990–91 recession. Figure 3.1 (page 12) shows the basis for this accusation by plotting both the Fed's target for the funds rate—its main monetary policy instrument—and the inflation rate (measured by the twelve-month trailing CPI) during the years 1990 through 1993. The difference between the two lines is thus the *real* federal funds rate, a reasonable measure of the tightness or ease of monetary policy.[1]

When the recession began in July 1990, the funds rate was at a high 8.25 percent—a rate the Fed had maintained since December 1989. The initial policy easing on July 13 turned out to be the first in a series of nine rate cuts over ten months that brought the funds rate down to 5.75 percent on the last day of April 1991—just a month after the recession trough. As the figure shows, the real funds rate over this period narrowed from over 3 percent to below 1 percent. After pausing for a few months but seeing few signs of vigorous growth, the Fed resumed cutting rates on August 6—taking the funds rate down to 4 percent by the end of the year. However, with inflation falling sharply during 1991, the real Fed funds rate declined much less (and, indeed, actually rose for part of that period). By year-end, the real Fed funds rate was still around 1 percent. The Fed then paused once again—for more than three months this time—to take the economy's pulse and to puzzle over why the recovery from recession was

11

FIGURE 3.1. THE FEDERAL FUNDS RATE AND CPI INFLATION

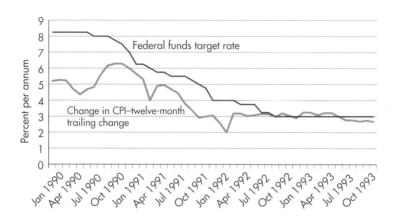

Source: Fed funds target rate from Board of Governors of the Federal Reserve System; CPI inflation from the U.S. Department of Labor, Bureau of Labor Statistics.

so weak. A final round of rate cuts brought the real funds rate down to roughly zero by July 1992.

In searching for explanations for why the economy was not responding to its medicine, the Fed eventually embraced the view that the U.S. economy was being restrained by a variety of stiff "headwinds," most of them financial. These included, most prominently, the weakened banking system and the decimated savings and loan industry, but also extended to overleveraged corporate balance sheets and heavily indebted consumers. Many critics at the time also suggested that bank supervisors—having been burned by the savings and loan debacle and castigated by Congress for being too lax—were forcing bankers to be excessively conservative by casting a jaundiced eye on all but the safest loans.[2]

The Fed's extreme caution about lowering rates in 1991 and early 1992 probably delayed a vigorous recovery, and may well have tipped the election to Bill Clinton; President George Bush certainly thought so. But what happened next is far more important to understanding what made the 1990s roar. The Fed held the funds rate at the extremely low level of 3 percent until February 1994. Since inflation was quite steady at roughly 3 percent during this period, the real funds rate was kept around zero for about a year and a half—providing an extraordinary dose of easy money. As Chairman Greenspan reflected at the September 1993 Federal Open Market Committee (FOMC) meeting, "We finally got it right and decided to sit with it."[3] Notice the adverb: *finally*.

How much stimulative effect did this medicine have? To answer this question quantitatively, we utilized two large macroeconometric models of the U.S. economy, the Fed's own FRB-US model and the proprietary WUMM model of Macroeconomic Advisers in St. Louis.[4] Both are fundamentally Keynesian models in which aggregate demand drives real output in the short run because prices and wages are sticky, and a Phillips curve mechanism drives wage and price inflation. The long-run properties of both models are basically classical, however, so real output is influenced by fiscal and monetary policy only temporarily. The two models differ greatly in their details (for example, in their treatments of expectations), including especially their respective dynamics.[5] While large-scale macroeconometric models like these can be (and are) used in forecasting, we believe they are best suited for simulation exercises—which is what we use them for in this book.

We used each model to compare actual history with a counterfactual simulation in which the federal funds rate never fell below 4 percent. Since the actual funds rate dipped below 4 percent in 1992:2 and remained there through 1994:2, this simulation amounted to holding the funds rate higher (by amounts ranging between 6 and 100 basis points) for nine quarters (1992:2 through 1994:2), and then matching history thereafter.[6] Table 3.1 (page 14) shows the results.

This table, like others to follow, displays the marginal effects of the change indicated in the title of the table (in this case, a tighter monetary policy) on three variables: the growth rate of real GDP, the inflation rate (measured by the CPI), and the level of the unemployment rate. Thus, for example, the upper left-hand number in the table means that, according to the WUMM model, real GDP would have grown 0.7 percentage point less during 1993 under the tighter monetary policy.

In appraising this and subsequent tables, it may be useful for the reader to know that, while monetary policy effects are larger in the FRB-US model, they take longer to build. The top two rows of Table 3.1 are an example of a pattern we will see over and over again. While the two models agree that, had the Fed not driven the funds rate all the way down to 3 percent, real GDP growth would have been about 0.7 percentage point lower in 1993 (that is, 1.8 percent growth instead of 2.5 percent), they differ thereafter. Depending on which model you believe, GDP growth during 1994 would have been either the same or 0.6 percent lower. Because of the slower growth (and consequently higher unemployment), inflation would have been reduced. If you cumulate the inflation reductions shown in the table, the price level winds up lower by 1.3 or 2.7 percent by 1996:4. The tighter monetary policy thus would have made a substantial difference, especially in the FRB-US model, which implies that the unemployment rate would have been 6.3 percent instead of 5.6 percent by late 1994.

TABLE 3.1. EFFECTS OF TIGHTER MONETARY POLICY IN 1992–94

DEVIATION FROM BASELINE	MODEL	1993:4	1994:4	1995:4	1996:4
Real GDP growth (Q4 over Q4)	WUMM	−0.7	0.0	0.3	−0.2
	FRB-US	−0.7	−0.6	−0.2	−0.3
CPI inflation rate (Q4 over Q4)	WUMM	0.0	−0.5	−0.5	−0.3
	FRB-US	−0.3	−0.6	−0.8	−1.0
Unemployment rate (difference)	WUMM	0.4	0.4	0.2	0.2
	FRB-US	0.4	0.7	0.7	0.9
Federal funds rate (difference)	Both	1.0	0.0	0.0	0.0

Source: Authors' calculations.

4.

THE FISCAL TURNING POINT

THE 1993 BUDGET AGREEMENT

On the fiscal front, the turning point came in 1993. During his successful campaign for the presidency in 1992, Bill Clinton seemed no more eager to tackle the nagging deficit problem than George Bush was. Neither campaign paid much more than lip service to the need for either significant tax increases or large cuts in expenditures—both of which were viewed as political losers. Bush, of course, was further burdened both by having reneged on his famous pledge, "Read my lips, no new taxes," and by the perceived failure of the 1990 budget agreement. Clinton, for his part, proposed spending cuts and tax increases on upper-income taxpayers. But he also promised both a variety of new spending initiatives and a tax cut for the middle class.

But during the November 1992–January 1993 transition period, the president-elect became convinced that reducing the budget deficit by cutting spending and raising taxes should be his overriding priority. Why? Economists at the time enunciated two main reasons to seek a smaller budget deficit.

The first was the traditional "crowding out" argument: that high budget deficits lead to high real interest rates, and therefore damage private investment spending. By reducing its deficit, economists argued, the government could boost investment, which would raise productivity and therefore real wages and living standards. Late in the decade, this argument would assume great prominence in the context of the interlocked debates over Social Security and paying down the national debt. But in 1992 and 1993, it did not resonate much

with politicians—and, in particular, not with Bill Clinton, who cor-
rectly perceived that voters cared about only three things: jobs, jobs,
and jobs.

Instead, a second, quite different argument likely persuaded
Clinton to opt for a major deficit reduction program: the fear that
some sort of financial calamity—perhaps imperiling the banking system as well as the stock and bond markets—might occur if the deficit
was not brought under control quickly. This collapse scenario had
more adherents on Wall Street than among academic economists—
which, of course, did not handicap it politically. In addition, and sig-
nificantly, Alan Greenspan was sympathetic. Since a financial
cataclysm would surely bring a recession in its wake, this scare story
rationalized portraying deficit reduction as a way to "save jobs."
Notice, however, that viewing deficit reduction as a net job creator
embodies a decidedly anti-Keynesian fiscal theory: that raising taxes
and/or reducing government spending *increases* output and employment. We will have much more to say about that later in this chapter.

Whatever his reasons, Clinton decided to take a big gamble—both
politically and economically—by making significant deficit reduction
his first major initiative.

The political risk was that Congress might reject his budget package, thereby hobbling the fledgling administration in its first months.
After all, Congress had demonstrated little appetite for either tax
increases or expenditure cuts over the preceding years. Despite much
subsequent criticism of President Clinton as a political opportunist, it
is hard to resist the conclusion that he chose major deficit reduction
in 1993 because he thought it was the right thing to do—and he was
willing to take the political heat. Either that, or he perceived that the
political tides were about to turn. For example, some observers claim
that the insurgent candidacy of Ross Perot in 1992 presaged such a
turn. In any event, the feared political disaster scenario very nearly
came to pass. The budget squeaked through Congress by one vote in
each chamber, without a single Republican supporter. Vice President
Al Gore's vote was needed to break a 50-50 tie in the Senate.

The economic risk was that the spending cuts and tax increases
would slow the economy unless either the Fed or the bond market
bailed the economy out with lower interest rates. Clinton was keenly
aware of both risks, but went ahead anyway.[1]

The economic plan that the new president presented with great
fanfare on February 17, 1993, followed a tortuous path through

Congress and was changed in hundreds of ways in the process.[2] Nonetheless, the budget package that eventually emerged from the legislative meat grinder in August 1993, though slightly bigger than Clinton's original proposal in terms of total deficit reduction, followed its broad contours.

The 1993 budget agreement galvanized the bond market, and the thirty-year bond rate plummeted by more than 160 basis points from Election Day 1992 to October 1993. While no one can ever be sure why markets react the way they do, the view that the bond market rally should be attributed to the markets' approval of the Clinton plan is buttressed by several facts.

First, contemporary observers saw it that way. Market commentary at the time focused on the deficit reduction plan as the principal—if not, indeed, the only—reason for the rally. At the July 1993 meeting of the FOMC (a month before the budget bill passed), Chairman Greenspan told his committee, "I don't know how much of the long-term interest rate reduction is attributable to the expectation that there will be a credible reduction in the deficit somewhere out there. I suspect most of it is, rightly or wrongly."[3]

Second, Figure 4.1 (page 18), which is based on a diagram that appeared in the February 1994 *Economic Report of the President*, offers a persuasive "event study" suggesting that news about the content and legislative progress of the president's proposal moved long-term bond rates sharply downward from January 1993 through August 1993. Notice that the bond rate started falling about a month after the election, as reports on what the new president was planning began to leak to the media. The decline in rates accelerated noticeably when the Clinton plan was introduced, when the House passed it (with many changes), and then again when the Senate and House approved the conference report.

Third, it is *not* true—as some have claimed—that the bond market rally in 1993 simply continued the trend toward lower long-term rates that had already been in progress for several years. In fact, the preceding multiyear decline in bond rates had come to a halt in January 1992, and, as Figure 4.1 shows, long rates moved up and down during the following year with no obvious trend. In fact, yields on long-term bonds were almost exactly the same in January 1993 as they had been a year earlier. The bond market did not begin rallying again until it started to hear leaks about the content of the Clinton budget proposal in December 1992.

FIGURE 4.1. YIELD ON TEN-YEAR CONSTANT MATURITY TREASURY SECURITIES: SEPTEMBER 1992–DECEMBER 1993

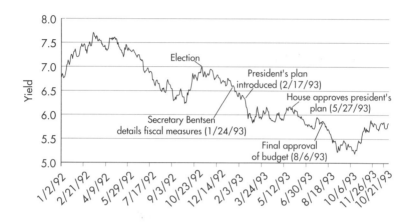

Source: Board of Governors of the Federal Reserve System.

So suppose that the 1993 budget agreement did indeed ignite the bond market rally. That raises at least two questions. First, did the observed declines in *nominal* interest rates constitute declines in *real* interest rates, or was it expected inflation that fell? While no one can ever be sure, we are inclined to attribute most of the lower nominal rates to falling real rates. In support of this view, the Blue Chip panel of professional economists' consensus forecasts of inflation—both the CPI and the GDP deflator—barely changed between January and August of 1993. But these are only short-run inflation forecasts, not the long-run inflationary expectations that are presumably relevant to bond rates.

The second, and much deeper, question is: How did the agreement so successfully win over the bond market vigilantes, a hard-bitten bunch who had grown quite cynical after years of "smoke-and-mirrors" budgets—and who were certainly not predisposed to trust a new Democratic government? We believe five factors contributed to the proposal's unusual and virtually instant credibility in the financial markets.

First, the Clinton budget package, which was originally advertised as $473 billion over five years (although the CBO scored it lower), took a far bolder line on deficit reduction than the market had been anticipating. As noted earlier, Clinton had not emphasized deficit reduction very much in his campaign. The proposal he submitted to Congress in February 1993 not only surprised markets by its large size but somehow also seemed to change the tenor of the political debate. Prior to February 17, 1993, raising taxes and cutting spending were viewed as sure political losers; deficit reduction had been dubbed "root-canal economics." But most of the rancorous battle from that day forward was over how to reduce the deficit even more than Clinton had proposed. How Bill Clinton transformed deficit reduction from a political sow's ear into a silk purse is something of a mystery. But he did it.[4]

Second, the new administration proved its seriousness of purpose by calling for significant tax increases—mainly higher personal income tax rates for upper-bracket taxpayers and a brand new tax on energy use (the ill-fated BTU tax). These decisions, made after George Bush had paid such a heavy political price for agreeing to a smaller tax hike, impressed the bond market. Notice in Figure 4.1 the sharp reaction on the day after Treasury Secretary Lloyd Bentsen "leaked" the administration's plan to propose an energy tax.

Third, the new administration pointedly rounded up some budgetary sacred cows for slaughter. Prominent among these was a modest reduction in Social Security benefits (accomplished by making more benefits taxable), thereby touching the alleged third rail of American politics. This, too, helped establish Clinton's *bona fides* as a serious deficit-cutter.

Fourth, the administration's first budget was remarkably free of the gimmicks and accounting subterfuges that the markets had come to expect, but grown to detest. Even Clinton's severest critics rarely if ever claimed that the package relied on smoke and mirrors to reduce the deficit. By common consent, the proposed cuts and tax hikes were real.[5] That earned the proposal some much needed credibility.

Fifth, the one gimmick that Clinton did adopt actually cut in the opposite direction: amazingly, the administration "cooked the books" against itself. Specifically, after a short but heated internal debate, the Clinton economic team decided to base its budget projections on the Congressional Budget Office's forecast, even though that forecast was more pessimistic than its own.[6] The president made this decision personally, knowing full well that by so doing he would not only raise the level of projected future deficits but also reduce the amount of deficit reduction he could claim for his program.

Together, these five aspects of the package seemed to imbue the Clinton program with a remarkable degree of credibility, especially considering the fact that the new administration had no track record. Interest rates tumbled immediately and sharply. (See again Figure 4.1.) The extent of the eventual bond market rally—more than 150 basis points from January to October of 1993—surprised virtually everyone. It also probably gave the economy a big lift, although no one would claim it was the only factor behind the investment boom.

How big a lift? We used the two econometric models mentioned earlier to simulate the effects of the bond market rally but, unfortunately, they give rather different answers—though mainly on timing. (See Table 4.1.) In each counterfactual simulation, we removed the rally by assuming that the yield on ten-year government bonds remained at its 1992:4 value (which was 6.74 percent) right through 1994:1—whereas in fact it fell as low as 5.61 percent. In the WUMM model, long bond rates have a strong, quick effect on GDP, but one that soon dissipates. The bond market rally therefore is estimated to have lowered the unemployment rate by a large 0.6 percentage point by 1994:4; but nothing is left by 1996:4. The effects of lower bond

TABLE 4.1. ESTIMATED EFFECTS OF 1993 BOND MARKET RALLY

DEVIATION FROM BASELINE	MODEL	1993:4	1994:4	1995:4	1996:4
Real GDP growth (Q4 over Q4)	WUMM	1.0	0.2	−0.5	−0.6
	FRB-US	0.6	0.7	0.0	−0.1
CPI inflation rate (Q4 over Q4)	WUMM	0.3	0.3	0.4	0.3
	FRB-US	0.1	0.1	0.1	0.5
Unemployment rate (difference)	WUMM	−0.3	−0.6	−0.3	0.0
	FRB-US	−0.1	−0.4	−0.6	−0.6
Yield on ten-year treasury bonds (difference)	Both	−1.13	0.00	0.00	0.00

Source: Authors' calculations.

yields build more slowly in the FRB-US model, but they last much longer. According to that model, rising bond prices reduced the 1994:4 unemployment rate by only 0.4 percentage point, but they cut the 1996:4 unemployment rate by 0.6 percentage point. The maximum effect on the *level* of real GDP is almost 1.5 percent in each model, but it comes about a year earlier in the WUMM—according to which the bond market rally added a full percentage point to the 1993 growth rate. These are not trivial impacts. In a word, the economy received a significant, though transitory, boost from the bond market.[7]

This episode raises a fascinating intellectual question: How, and under what circumstances, can what we normally think of as contractionary fiscal policy really be expansionary? One view common among macroeconomists these days holds that monetary policy can and does offset the effects of any fiscal action on aggregate demand, thereby rendering fiscal changes neither expansionary nor contractionary. On that view, the Clinton deficit reduction program should not have been expected to cause a slump. But neither should it have precipitated a boom.

So consider a hybrid theory that, while admittedly impure, may be more empirically relevant to the events of 1993. Specifically, suppose that:[8]

1. Long-term interest rates are the appropriate weighted average of expected future short-term rates—the so-called expectations theory of the term structure.

2. The short rate in each period is jointly determined by the Fed's monetary policy (which fixes the supply schedule of bank reserves) and the level of nominal demand (which determines the position of the demand schedule).

3. The announced fiscal change pertains to the future, not to the present. So it has no immediate effect on spending.

4. Market participants expect the central bank to offset the effects of future fiscal policy on aggregate demand.

Under these assumptions, a credibly promised future tax increase or expenditure cut could, ceteris paribus, lead markets to expect a different policy mix in the future—easier money and tighter fiscal policy—with no net effect on aggregate demand. That should mean lower expected future short rates, but no slump. The expectations theory of the term structure will then telescope these lower expected future short rates into lower long-term interest rates today, which will stimulate the economy.

While this story is coherent, it is not entirely consistent with the events of 1993. For example, it assumes that the Fed was prepared to offset the effects of fiscal policy on future demand, but somehow would not offset the effects on current demand. After all, at least some of the negative impact of the Clinton deficit reduction plan on spending came immediately, as did the bond market rally. Why would the Fed not offset this? One possible answer is that the Fed was having trouble stimulating the economy and therefore welcomed any assist it could get from the bond market. That is probably true. But it throws a bit of cold water on the facile notion that the Fed controls aggregate demand on a period-by-period basis. And besides, as we will see shortly, there are repeated references in the 1993 FOMC minutes to the possible depressing effects of the deficit reduction program on aggregate demand—plus a few to the stimulative effects of the lower bond rates that the deficit reduction program may have engendered.

Furthermore, at least some contemporary observers, especially Republicans who opposed the Clinton plan, predicted that the tax hikes would lead to recession. That, the critics argued, is why long-term interest rates went down. But these naysayers were not only quite wrong, they were a tiny minority group: the Blue Chip consensus forecast for real growth in 1994 stood at 2.8 percent in August 1993 (when the budget agreement passed), which at that time was a forecast for above-trend growth.

Another theory that is carelessly tossed about holds that lowering the expected future path of the national debt reduces the "risk premium" on government bond rates. This notion probably makes sense for many countries, especially those that finance their public debt in foreign currencies. But when we think about applying it to the United States, what, precisely, is the risk that deficit reduction reduces? Default on the national debt? That hardly seems plausible for the United States. Future inflation? That depends on the Fed's propensity to monetize deficits, which appears to be very low. And, in any case, a rise in inflationary expectations might raise *nominal* interest rates but lower *real* interest rates.

One possible answer to this question harks back to the financial collapse scenario we discussed earlier. Suppose the risk that markets fear is that a rising national debt (especially one that is rising faster than GDP) might eventually lead to a financial cataclysm. Then deflecting the path of the debt downward may alleviate such concerns and therefore lower the risk premiums built into real interest rates.

Last, there is a decidedly nonrational expectations possibility. Suppose the markets expected the Clinton program to cause a slump later on, but the Fed surprised everyone by preventing the slump from occurring. Then expectations of a future recession could have stimulated the economy in 1993 by provoking a bond market rally, even though no actual slump ever arrived. However, anyone who uses this theory to explain the events that followed August 1993 must answer the following difficult question: When, exactly, did the Fed ease monetary policy by enough to avert a recession? Remember, the Fed held rates steady throughout 1993, and then raised them aggressively between February 1994 and February 1995.

Our own favorite explanation is that an unusual coincidence of timing and policy conspired to change market psychology fundamentally. The time was right: Clinton's election marked the end of the twelve-year Reagan-Bush presidency, and change was expected. So both the public and the markets were receptive. And the policy was right: the budget package had the market-pleasing features we outlined earlier. So the bond market rallied strongly. Needless to say, this is not a formula that can be repeated at will. Lower bond rates, in turn, ignited the economy. The Fed watched all this happen for a while, somewhat surprised by the large reaction, and then decided to rein in demand.

In this regard, another interesting counterfactual question arises: Did the Clinton deficit reduction program induce an easier monetary policy by pushing back the date when the Fed would finally remove its foot from the monetary accelerator and start raising interest rates? Such a delay could have happened for either economic or political reasons. The political reason is clear: central bankers who abhor large budget deficits may want to reward politicians for good behavior. In some sense, both Greenspan and Paul Volcker before him had been "offering" the politicians this deal for years. The economic reason is also straightforward: a fiscal contraction will naturally lead a stabilizing central bank to pursue an easier monetary policy. However, in this case, the bond market rally gave the economy a strong push forward, which the Fed may have felt obliged to counter.

Did this happen in the United States in 1993–94? Implicitly, it may have. But a close reading of the verbatim FOMC transcripts for 1993 uncovers only scattered mentions of the thought that a tighter fiscal policy ought to call forth a looser monetary policy. For example, in the March 1993 meeting, Robert Parry, president of the Federal Reserve Bank of San Francisco, observed, "Most of the people who have looked at the Clinton program contend that it's going to produce weakness over the next several years."[9] Making the link more explicit at the May meeting, Governor John LaWare asserted, "It can't have escaped any reasonably intelligent observer that the [budget] proposals . . . are essentially contractive. A premature move to tighten policy against that background could be disastrous to economic growth and could run the risk of [reducing] enthusiasm for . . . budget discipline."[10]

But other FOMC members were either thinking about the implications of the bond market rally or were wary of tying monetary policy decisions too closely to fiscal policy. At the February 1993 meeting, when substantial deficit reduction was expected but had not yet been proposed by the White House (and the bond market was rallying on the rumors), Vice Chairman David Mullins cautioned that "even if we had this credible deficit reduction package and long rates fell, it's not clear that we should respond by lowering short rates because we could have a . . . stimulative impact of a fall in long rates."[11] In September, after the package had been enacted into law, President Jerry Jordan of the Cleveland Federal Reserve Bank warned against adopting "a monetary policy in the future that is different than it would have been in absence of the fiscal package" because in that case "monetary policy is being adjusted because of the fiscal regime."[12]

On balance, the FOMC transcripts do not provide much support for the view that fiscal discipline prolonged the period of easy money. Nonetheless, Greenspan allegedly told President Clinton some years later that "If you had not turned the fiscal situation around, we couldn't have had the kind of monetary policy we've had."[13] In any case, the facts remain: the Fed's period of extraordinarily easy money lasted into early 1994, and the first Clinton budget represented a substantial tightening of fiscal policy. The sharp swing in the fiscal-monetary policy mix was under way.

5.

THE FED ENGINEERS A
SOFT LANDING, 1994–96

By the winter of 1993–94, the economy had been growing strongly for two years or more,[1] the unemployment rate was down to about 6.5 percent and falling, and the Fed decided it was time to raise the real federal funds rate above zero. While its first rate hike did not come until early February, a consensus that rates would be going up had developed in the FOMC a few months earlier. By the time of its December 1993 meeting, six of the nineteen committee members already thought the Fed should start raising rates immediately—and two of them dissented against Chairman Alan Greenspan's recommendation to wait a bit longer.[2] This hawkish attitude marked a big change from the November meeting, when virtually no one had objected to Greenspan's recommendation to stay put. The Fed was plainly chomping at the bit.

And not without reason. The economy was growing well above what was then believed to be the trend growth rate, and contemporary estimates of the output gap suggested there was not much slack left.[3] Yet the real federal funds rate was still fixed at zero—indicative of an extremely loose monetary policy stance. Overshooting seemed a real possibility in such an environment, even though inflation was not rising, and the Fed decided to make what it called a "preemptive strike" against incipient inflation.

In fact, it was a foregone conclusion that rates would go up at the February 1994 FOMC meeting, and Greenspan had to press unusually hard to restrain the committee from raising the funds rate even more. Transcripts of FOMC meetings are normally deadly dull—just try reading one—but this meeting had real drama. Greenspan opened the normal policy roundtable by proposing a 25 basis point increase in the federal funds rate coupled with a symmetric directive. But by the time ten of the other sixteen members had spoken,[4] only four had registered support for Greenspan's recommendation; six wanted to go up by 50 basis points instead. Alarmed, the Fed chairman interrupted the roundtable to try to stem the tide: "I will tell you that if we do 50 basis points today, we have a very high probability of cracking these markets. I think that would be a very unwise procedure."[5] This was a highly unusual intervention on Greenspan's part in the midst of the go-round. Yet only two of the remaining six FOMC members were persuaded to side with him—leaving the final "straw poll" at ten votes for 50 basis points and only seven (including the chairman's) for 25 basis points.

At this point, Greenspan really cracked the whip, virtually insisting on a unanimous vote in favor of his proposal. He declared: "I would be very concerned if this committee went 50 basis points now because I don't think the markets expect it. . . . I am telling you—and I've seen these markets—this is not the time to do this. . . . I really request that we not do this. . . . I would also be concerned if this Committee were not in concert because at this stage we . . . are going to have to do things which the rest of the world is not going to like. . . . If we are perceived to be split . . . , I think we're risking some very serious problems for this organization."[6] Then, in one of the most misleading "unanimous" votes in FOMC history, every member of the FOMC voted to support its chairman's recommendation.

At the White House, President Clinton was livid that Greenspan and his colleagues would have the temerity to raise interest rates just six months after his painful deficit reduction program had passed. But administration economists saw rate hikes as both inevitable and appropriate; the only questions were when they would start and how high rates would go. They counseled Clinton not to browbeat the Fed publicly, and Clinton scrupulously heeded the advice—beginning a hands-off-the-Fed policy that was to continue, virtually without exception, throughout the Clinton presidency. Few if any previous presidents have cut the Fed such slack.

In this context, it is important to note that the Fed's goal in 1994 was not to push the economy below full employment in an aggressive attempt to pull inflation down. In fact, FOMC hawks complained repeatedly that the committee was contenting itself with stabilizing, rather than lowering, the inflation rate—a policy they thought inappropriate.[7] But Greenspan and the FOMC majority were seeking to achieve a so-called soft landing at about full employment (say, an unemployment rate of 6 percent), as depicted in Figure 5.1. If successful, the Fed would stabilize inflation more or less where it was—about 3 percent.

FIGURE 5.1. A SOFT LANDING

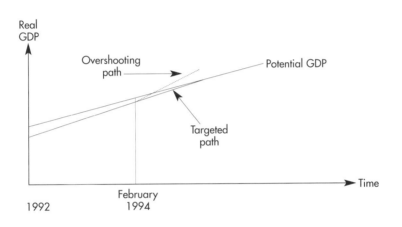

In other words, the Fed sought to move the real federal funds rate up to its "neutral" value.[8] But what rate was neutral? Greenspan kicked off a considerable public debate over precisely that question when he explicitly mentioned the concept—without offering a number, of course—in his explanation of the Fed's initial rate hike. The Fed itself wondered at first whether the neutral real rate might be as low as 1 percent, which would mean a 4 percent nominal funds rate.[9] But one thing was clear: when it started raising rates, the FOMC had no clear notion of where the neutral rate might be. At the March 1994 FOMC meeting, Greenspan suggested a 4 to 4.5 percent nominal rate.[10] By July, the staff estimate of the neutral (nominal) funds rate was up to about 5.25 percent.[11] But President William McDonough of the New York Federal Reserve suggested at the September meeting that a 4.75 percent rate (the rate at the time) was neutral.[12] Such estimates, which placed the neutral nominal rate in the 4.25 to 5.25 percent range (hence about 1.25 to 2.25 percent in real terms), seem to reflect an appropriate range of uncertainty. This important parameter is simply not known.

There are two apparent ways to estimate the neutral real federal funds rate. The first method applies the definition directly, by solving an econometric model explicitly for the real short rate that will stabilize inflation, given the level of other relevant variables. Such a calculation, of course, is sensitive to the details of the model, and different models will give different answers. It also implies that a variety of other variables, such as government spending and exports, affect the neutral interest rate. So the neutral rate moves around a great deal. A study by a Fed staff economist using the Federal Reserve Board's own model estimated that the funds rate was only slightly below neutral before the Fed started tightening monetary policy in 1994, and then rose to neutral early in 1994—more or less what Greenspan believed early in the tightening cycle (but disbelieved later).[13]

The second method uses historical data to calculate the long-run average *ex post* real rate. On the assumption that monetary policy must have been neutral on average over periods as long as thirty to forty years, that should approximate the long-run average neutral rate (though not the neutral rate of any particular time period).[14] This method tends to produce estimates of the neutral real rate around 2 percent, depending on the exact time period used. For example, the real federal funds rate, defined as the nominal federal funds rate less the four-quarter trailing CPI inflation rate, averaged 2.3 percent between the first quarter of 1960 and the fourth quarter of 1993. The range of plausible estimates left by these two methods led one of us (Blinder), while vice chairman of the Fed in 1994, to enunciate a likely range for the neutral real Fed funds rate between 1.75 percent and 2.75 percent, implying a nominal funds rate around 4.75 to 5.75 percent. If neutrality was the FOMCs target, the 100-basis-point range left it with plenty of room for disagreements over monetary policy.

During 1994 and 1995, various Federal Reserve officials repeatedly warned the markets and the public of the difficulty of achieving a perfect soft landing. Doing so would require the Fed not only to guesstimate the neutral interest rate fairly accurately, but also to arrive at that rate with just about the right timing (given the long lags in monetary policy). To do this, the Fed would have to be lucky as well as skillful. If a major shock to aggregate demand or supply occurred during the Fed's fine-tuning operation, even the best-laid plans would go awry. In the event, the Fed ultimately raised interest rates seven times over the course of a year, by a total of 300 basis points—bringing the funds rate to 6 percent on February 1, 1995, when the tightening cycle stopped. (Figure 5.2 shows the path of the federal funds rate during this tightening phase and its subsequent evolution.) This seemed to do the job, though the final rate hikes in this series, 75 basis points in November 1994 and 50 basis points in February 1995, were highly contentious.

At the time of the November 1994 meeting, the funds rate was at 4.75 percent, and the financial markets were clamoring for much higher rates to stave off inflation. However, several FOMC members (including the authors of this book) began to voice concerns that the Fed might engage in "overkill" by underestimating the lags in monetary policy. The committee voted unanimously to raise the funds rate by 75 basis points—the only move of that magnitude in the entire Greenspan era. But several members expressed a preference for going up by only 50 basis points, and others made it clear that they disagreed with the staff's view that 150 basis points of additional

FIGURE 5.2. FEDERAL FUNDS TARGET RATE, 1994–2000

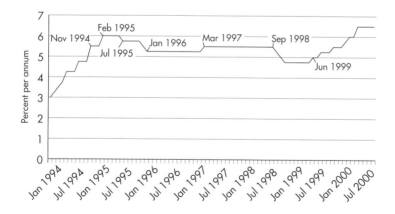

Source: Board of Governors of the Federal Reserve System.

tightening—which would have taken the funds rate to a peak of 6.25 percent—would eventually be needed.

The Fed's final rate hike of 50 basis points came at the January 31–February 1, 1995, meeting, even though several FOMC members (especially the authors of this book) voiced concerns that the Fed might be raising rates too precipitously. Around that time, the economy was just starting to show indications of slowing down. As Greenspan put it, "There are now tentative signs, not necessarily persuasive but definitely beginning to appear, of slight cracks along the road."[15] In addition, U.S. exports were clearly poised to decline in the aftermath of the Mexican financial crisis. Since the traditional inventory accelerator mechanism could be expected to exacerbate any slowdown in spending, the danger of a hard landing was rising.[16] Although financial markets were still clamoring for more tightening, Greenspan noted, "It is by no means evident that, if this cracking that we have seen continues, . . . there will be another tightening of policy."[17]

As the year progressed, the danger of monetary overkill became a concern of the FOMC. Fortunately, long-term interest rates played a stabilizing role during this episode, as they did later in the expansion.[18] Even before the Fed's final rate hike in February 1995, the yield on the thirty-year Treasury bond had declined about 40 basis points from its November 1994 high. This drop in long-term rates probably reflected the market's perception that signs of a slowdown were emerging—prompting a reevaluation of the amount of tightening the Fed would have to do. In the following months, long-term rates fell further as evidence of a slowdown accumulated, dropping from 7.75 percent on February 1 to 6.61 percent on July 5, 1995, the day before the FOMC's first rate cut.

Statements by Fed officials reinforced the market's reassessment of the likely future stance of policy. Three weeks after the Fed raised rates on February 1, 1995, Greenspan hinted at the possibility of a preemptive strike against a downturn when he noted in congressional testimony that "there may come a time when we hold our policy stance unchanged, or even ease, despite adverse price data, should we see signs that underlying forces are acting ultimately to reduce inflation pressures."[19] Between July 1995 and January 1996, the FOMC finally validated market expectations by reducing the federal funds rate from 6 percent to 5.25 percent in three steps. In the view of some observers, this shifted monetary policy from mildly restrictive to approximately neutral, although an alternative interpretation of the rate cuts is that they merely kept the real federal funds rate from rising in the face of declining inflationary expectations.

The prospective impact of more contractionary fiscal policy also affected monetary policy decisions, at least in the eyes of some FOMC members (including the authors), reinforcing the desirability of bringing the Fed funds rate down. An agreement between the administration and the new Republican-led Congress to balance the budget via another round of budget cuts was widely anticipated and was discussed in the FOMC.[20] Macroeconometric model simulations at the time suggested that the ensuing fiscal restraint might lower the equilibrium real federal funds rate by 150 basis points, a very large amount.

By the end of 1995, it appeared that the Fed had defied the odds and achieved the elusive soft landing at full employment. The unemployment rate was 5.6 percent, which was considered a rather optimistic estimate of the nonaccelerating inflation rate of unemployment (NAIRU) at the time; the GDP growth rate in the second half of 1995 was 3.2 percent;[21] and the core inflation rate (twelve-month trailing core CPI) was still 3 percent. It was this stunningly successful episode, we believe, that elevated Greenspan's already lofty reputation to that of macroeconomic magician. From that point until recently, it seemed the Fed could do no wrong in the market's eyes.

But how, precisely, did the Fed's fine-tuning exercise affect GDP growth? To answer that question, we again utilized the WUMM and FRB-US models to simulate the path of the U.S. economy under alternative monetary policies. This time we considered two. The first alternative embodies a looser monetary policy: it asks what would have happened if the Fed had held the federal funds rate at 3 percent right through the first half of 1995. While this is not a serious policy option that anyone would have entertained, it does provide a gross measure of the Fed's (negative) impact on GDP and other variables.[22] The second assumes a tighter monetary policy: it asks how different things would have been if the Fed had listened to the more hawkish market sentiment that prevailed in late 1994 and kept pushing rates higher, reaching a 7.5 percent funds rate by the May 1995 meeting.

Table 5.1 (page 32) presents the three different paths for the federal funds rate. Tables 5.2 (page 32) and 5.3 (page 33) summarize the simulation results for the looser and tighter alternatives.

Under the easier monetary policy, the economy grows substantially faster in 1994 (in both models) and 1995 (sharply faster in

TABLE 5.1. FEDERAL FUNDS RATE UNDER
THREE DIFFERENT MONETARY POLICIES

QUARTER	1994				1995				1996
	1	2	3	4	1	2	3	4	1
Looser	3.00	3.00	3.00	3.00	3.00	3.00	3.75	4.50	5.25
Actual	3.21	3.94	4.49	5.17	5.81	6.02	5.80	5.72	5.36
Tighter	3.21	3.94	4.49	5.23	6.50	7.35	6.68	6.02	5.36

Source: Authors' calculations.

1995 in the FRB-US model). By the end of 1995, real GDP is 2.6 or
3.9 percent above baseline in the two models. In both models, unemployment falls further and faster—reaching 4.0 or 4.3 percent by the
end of 1995—and inflation rises by about 1 percent above its historical level—to a bit above 4 percent in 1996. (See Table 5.2.) In the
WUMM model, the delayed monetary tightening produces a pretty
hard landing: the numbers in the table imply that real growth would
have slowed to barely above zero during 1996 and unemployment
would have reached 6.3 percent by 1997:3.

TABLE 5.2. ESTIMATED EFFECTS OF EASIER
MONETARY POLICY DURING 1994–95

DEVIATION FROM BASELINE	MODEL	1994:4	1995:4	1996:4	1997:4
Real GDP growth (Q4 over Q4)	WUMM	2.0	0.6	−3.8	−1.4
	FRB-US	1.2	2.7	−1.3	−1.2
CPI Inflation Rate (Q4 over Q4)	WUMM	0.1	0.1	0.9	0.2
	FRB-US	0.2	0.9	1.2	2.1
Unemployment rate (difference)	WUMM	−0.6	−1.3	0.3	1.5
	FRB-US	−0.4	−1.6	−1.7	−1.1
Yield on ten-year treasury bonds (difference)	WUMM	−1.84	1.21	2.06	−0.58
	FRB-US	−1.84	1.21	2.06	0.00

Source: Authors' calculations.

TABLE **5.3**. ESTIMATED EFFECTS OF TIGHTER
MONETARY POLICY DURING **1994–95**

DEVIATION FROM BASELINE	MODEL	1994:4	1995:4	1996:4	1997:4
Real GDP growth (Q4 over Q4)	WUMM	0.0	–0.6	0.0	0.1
	FRB-US	0.0	–0.5	–0.3	–0.1
CPI inflation rate (Q4 over Q4)	WUMM	0.0	0.1	–0.3	–0.3
	FRB-US	0.0	–0.2	–0.3	–0.4
Unemployment rate (difference)	WUMM	0.0	0.2	0.3	0.2
	FRB-US	0.0	0.2	0.4	0.4
Yield on ten-year treasury bonds (difference)	WUMM	0.02	0.37	0.02	0.14
	FRB-US	0.01	0.20	0.06	0.02

Source: Authors' calculations.

The tighter monetary policy scenario (see Table 5.3) naturally produces effects that go in the opposite direction. Growth is about one-half percent slower during 1995; unemployment is 0.2 or 0.4 percentage point higher during 1995–97, and inflation is roughly 0.3 percentage point lower during 1996 and 1997. Together, these two simulations agree with the market's view that the Fed threaded the needle pretty well in the 1994–96 episode. The tightening in 1994–95 certainly should not have been delayed, and it does not appear to have been excessive. The easing in 1995–96 might have been judged a bit too permissive at the time, but the wisdom of hindsight belies that view.

6.

THE FED FORBEARS AND THE PHILLIPS CURVE COOPERATES

The state of the U.S. economy looked superb at the start of 1996, and it just kept getting better over the ensuing years. The unemployment rate belied the popular view that the NAIRU was between 5.5 percent and 6 percent by falling steadily right through 1999. By December 1999, unemployment stood at 4.1 percent, its lowest level in twenty-nine years.[1] Real GDP growth averaged 4.5 percent during these four years—well in excess of contemporaneous estimates of potential output growth. And yet (as Figure 5.2 shows, page 29), aside from one minor upward adjustment of 25 basis points in March 1997, the federal funds rate was not raised again until June 1999.

Thus, apart from its reaction to the 1998 financial crisis, the best one-word description of the Fed's monetary policy from early 1996 to the summer of 1999 is *forbearance*. The FOMC watched, scratched its collective head in a struggle to understand the forces restraining inflation, worried that the good luck would soon end and inflation would again rear its ugly head, but largely held its fire. In fact, the Fed actually cut the funds rate by 75 basis points to combat growing international turmoil during the worldwide financial crisis in the fall of 1998.

One important question for macro-historians is why the Fed chose to forbear even as the unemployment rate drifted down to levels that previously had been associated with accelerating inflation. Part of the answer is simply that, despite the inflation fears of FOMC hawks and many outside forecasters, the worst never came to pass. As Table 6.1 (page 36) illustrates, inflation did not rise; on the contrary, it fell.

TABLE 6.1. MEASURES OF CONSUMER PRICE INFLATION
(TWELVE-MONTH OR FOUR-QUARTER TRAILING CHANGE)

	LAST MONTH OR QUARTER OF					
	1994	1995	1996	1997	1998	1999
CPI-U	2.7	2.5	3.3	1.7	1.6	2.7
PCE, chain weighted	2.1	2.1	2.3	1.5	1.1	2.0
CPI-U-RS	2.3	2.4	3.0	1.6	1.4	2.7
Core CPI-U	2.6	3.0	2.6	2.2	2.4	1.9
Core PCE, chain weighted	2.3	2.3	1.8	1.7	1.6	1.5
Core CPI-U-RS	2.2	2.8	2.4	2.1	2.2	2.0

Source: All CPI-U and CPI-U-RS data are from the U.S. Department of Labor, Bureau of Labor Statistics; PCE data are from the U.S. Department of Commerce, Bureau of Economic Analysis.

The table displays the behavior of three broad-based measures of consumer prices from 1994 to 1999: the consumer price index for all urban consumers (CPI-U), the chain-weighted price index for personal consumption expenditures,[2] and a new research series—the CPI-U-RS, which is an estimate of the (hypothetical) rate of inflation in the CPI-U under the methodology in place as of 1999. The core versions of each index, which exclude food and energy prices, were mostly declining during this period. The fact that core inflation was falling while unemployment was so extraordinarily low surprised both the FOMC and outside observers. The Blue Chip forecasters, for example, regularly overestimated inflation in 1996, 1997, and 1998. Similarly, official inflation forecasts from the White House, the Congressional Budget Office (CBO), and the Fed were routinely too pessimistic about both inflation and real growth.

A major puzzle—perhaps *the* major puzzle—about this entire period is why inflation remained so low after 1995. The leading candidate (or candidates) is a series of disinflationary "supply shocks." FOMC discussions dating back to 1995 focused on the moderation in employee benefits due to health care restructuring and the possible role of worker insecurity as factors restraining compensation increases. Productivity developments also attracted some attention, especially from Alan Greenspan, even though the evidence for productivity improvement was mainly anecdotal or indirect at the time.[3] During 1997, the behavior of oil and nonoil import prices was added to the FOMC's list of pertinent supply shocks.

The following simple wage-price model provides a useful framework for organizing our discussion of these favorable shocks:

(1) $\dot{w} = x^w + \pi^e + f(U - U^*) + z_1 + error$

(2) $\pi = \dot{w} - x^f + z_2 + error$

Equation (1) is a standard Phillips curve: the rate of increase of nominal labor compensation ($\dot{w}$) depends on the growth rate of productivity (x), expected inflation π^e, the deviation of unemployment (U) from its natural rate (U^*), and "shocks" to the wage equation (z_1). (The stochastic error terms in the two equations are inessential here and will be ignored.) Equation (2) is a conventional markup equation: prices rise at the same rate as unit labor costs ($\dot{w} - x$), except when shocks to the price equation (z_2)—such as food or energy prices—perturb this relationship. The superscripts on the productivity growth rates in each equation—w for worker and f for firm—are important, and will be explained presently.

Solving (1) and (2) together, and using lagged inflation as a crude proxy for expected inflation, yields what is often called the price-price Phillips curve:

(3) $\pi - \pi_{-1} = x^w - x^f + f(U - U^*) + z_1 + z_2 + errors$

Equation (3) says that the normal relationship between unemployment and *changes* in inflation (or, if you reject the proxy, *unexpected* inflation) can be perturbed by wage shocks (z_1), price shocks (z_2), and any deviation between the productivity growth rates perceived by workers and firms ($x^w - x^f$). In addition, the NAIRU (U^*) might change. In what follows, we will pay some attention to each of these four possible explanations for why inflation remained so low in the 1995–99 period.[4]

But first it is worth looking at Figure 6.1 (page 38), which uses data for the 1960–99 period to illustrate the gross relationship between unemployment and changes in inflation—without controlling for any of the other factors in equation (3).[5] The figure embodies an extremely simple theory of changes in inflation—after all, it allows for no other variables. Nonetheless, it fits the data better than might be expected. It also shows, perhaps surprisingly, that inflation

FIGURE 6.1. UNEMPLOYMENT AND THE
CHANGE IN CPI INFLATION, 1960–99

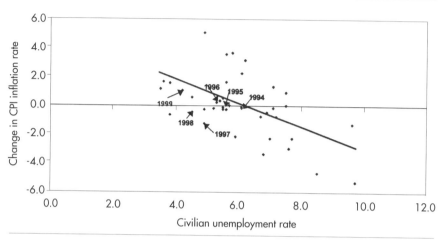

Note: Regression line based on 1960–95 data.

Source: U.S. Department of Labor, Bureau of Labor Statistics.

performance was not very exceptional during the 1994–96 period but was unusually low during 1998 and, especially, 1997. Bearing this in mind, we proceed now to some explanations.

SURPRISINGLY MODERATE WAGE INFLATION

We begin with wage shocks (z_1). Equations like (3) tracked the data quite well while the Fed was piloting the economy to a soft landing in 1994–95. Indeed, one of us (Blinder) at the time dubbed the excellent fit of the (price-price) Phillips curve "the clean little secret of macroeconometrics."[6] But, if you peered below the surface, trouble was brewing: wages were coming in lower than expected and markups higher. Though the errors were not huge, they were notably one-sided. The econometric puzzle was twofold: Why was compensation growing so slowly given the apparent tightness of the labor market? And why, given the slow growth of labor costs, wasn't inflation falling more?

We can think of two plausible—and related—explanations, both of which were much discussed at the time. According to what might be called the "traumatized worker hypothesis," after being terrorized by corporate restructuring, suffering through a recession, and then struggling through an initially "jobless" recovery, American workers became more concerned with job security than with real wage increases.[7] Think of the traumatized worker hypothesis as either a decrease in U^* or a negative z_1 shock, possibly accompanied by a positive z_2 shock, as bargaining power shifts from labor to management. Greenspan himself called attention to this idea in numerous speeches, adding the further point that more rapid technological progress also increased insecurity by quickening the pace at which job skills become obsolete.[8] An even stronger version of the theory would suggest that American labor suffered not just a temporary trauma, but actually saw its bargaining position eroded on a permanent (or at least long-lasting) basis.

Evidence supporting this hypothesis was mixed. Some survey results indicated that levels of job insecurity were unusually high given the unemployment rate, but some did not.[9] Again controlling for the state of the labor market, the data seemed to show low levels of voluntary quits and high levels of job loss—both indicators of insecurity.[10] And work stoppages were also at forty-five-year lows.[11]

A second hypothesis starts with the observation that fringe benefits, which had been rising faster than wages and salaries for years, decelerated sharply in 1993 and 1994—and actually grew slower than wages starting in 1995. (See Figure 6.2, page 40.) One can think of this event as a negative "benefits shock," though we do not necessarily mean to imply by that label that it was some sort of an exogenous event. It could be that the downward deflection of benefit costs was the way the market happened to register some deeper phenomenon— such as a decline in labor's bargaining power.

Decelerating health insurance costs were the best-known part of the benefits story and were certainly of substantial importance. Medical care cost inflation, which had skyrocketed into double digits in the late 1980s, began to de-escalate early in the 1990s. Cost increases for group health insurance began to abate in 1993 and 1994 and actually turned negative during 1995–98. Substantial restructuring took place in the health care sector in the aftermath of the failed Clinton initiative, and employers shifted workers out of fee-for-service and into managed care plans. Part of the decline reflected decreases in coverage, increases in copayments and deductibles, and the like.[12] Figure 6.3 (page 41) shows the behavior of employers' costs for private

FIGURE 6.2. CHANGES IN WAGES AND SALARIES AND
BENEFITS IN THE EMPLOYMENT COST INDEX

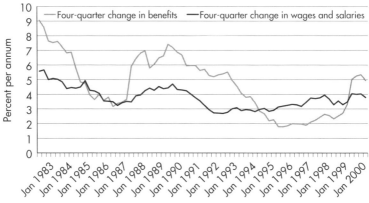

Source: U.S. Department of Labor, Bureau of Labor Statistics.

group health insurance per hour of work in the nonfarm business sector. These costs grew by 7.4 percent per year between 1990 and 1994, then *declined* at an average 2.3 percent per year during 1995–98. That was a stunning turnaround.

But health insurance was not the whole story. Figure 6.3 also shows that employer contributions for pensions and retirement benefits plummeted, as the soaring stock market allowed firms to pay much less into their defined-benefit retirement plans. The costs of workers' compensation also fell.[13] In other words, workers "took their hit" mainly in the benefits component of total compensation rather than in the wage component.

A simple calculation suggests that this containment of employee benefit costs could have translated into a substantial decline in the inflation rate of overall compensation. During 1992–94, employee benefit costs (excluding employers' contributions for social insurance) per hour of work rose 1.4 percent per annum more rapidly than an index of nonfarm business prices. During 1995–98, these benefit costs actually *declined* by 4.4 percent per year relative to this same price index. Although these fringe benefits account for only about 10 percent of total compensation, the 5.8 percentage point

FIGURE 6.3. GROWTH IN EMPLOYERS' HOURLY
COST FOR SELECTED PRIVATE BENEFITS[a]

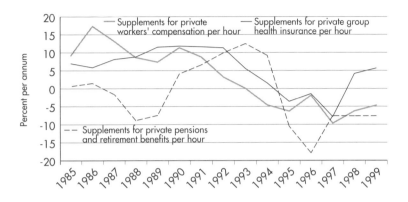

[a] Supplements divided by hours of work in the nonfarm business sector.

Source: Supplements from U.S. Department of Commerce, Bureau of Economic Analysis; hours from U.S. Department of Labor, Bureau of Labor Statistics.

reduction in the growth rate of real hourly benefit costs, other things equal, should have reduced the pace of compensation growth by about 0.5 percentage point.

But wait. Doesn't economic theory suggest that market forces determine the growth rate of total compensation, not just wages? The answer is, yes. So in the long run, wages and salaries should accelerate to offset any slowdown in benefits.[14] However, this one-to-one offset need not appear in the short run. When workers are not pressing very hard for higher compensation or when firms are successfully resisting labor's demands, companies that manage to economize on benefit costs may be able to pocket the gains for a while. In fact, labor's share of nonfarm business output fell by a remarkable four percentage points between 1992 and 1997, reaching its lowest level in the postwar period, which is consistent with the view that workers lost out. Profit margins and the return to capital naturally increased.[15]

To assess the impact of lower benefit costs on the economy, we again used the WUMM and FRB-US macroeconometric models. Specifically, we asked how different economic performance would

have been if hourly employer costs for fringe benefits had continued to increase at a rate 1.4 percentage points faster than the index
of nonfarm business prices in 1995–99—just as they had in
1992–94.[16] Since faster growth of fringe benefits would raise inflation, it is hardly plausible that the Federal Reserve would have
held the nominal federal funds rate constant in such an environment. So our simulations assumed the Fed would have kept the
real federal funds rate constant, adjusting the nominal funds rate
point for point with inflation. The results, which are reported in
Table 6.2, suggest that slower growth of benefit costs had a large
economic impact. In both models, the "benefits shock" lowers
price inflation by an average of almost one percentage point during
1995–98, even though unemployment is reduced substantially.[17]
These are sizable effects, bigger than the simple back-of-the-envelope
calculation suggests. Why?

In the FRB-US model, nominal wage bargains depend on expected inflation. The benefits shock kicks off a virtuous circle in
which lower inflation in one year reduces expected future inflation,
nominal wage increases, and therefore actual inflation in subsequent

TABLE 6.2. THE EFFECTS OF SLOWER GROWTH IN REAL
EMPLOYEE BENEFIT COSTS AFTER 1994
(REAL FEDERAL FUNDS RATE HELD AT BASELINE LEVEL)

DEVIATION FROM BASELINE	MODEL	1995:4	1996:4	1997:4	1998:4	1999:4
Real GDP growth (Q4 over Q4)	WUMM	0.2	1.0	1.0	0.1	–0.4
	FRB-US	0.0	0.2	0.3	0.4	0.1
CPI inflation rate (Q4 over Q4)	WUMM	–0.8	–1.3	–1.5	–0.7	–0.3
	FRB-US	–0.2	–0.7	–1.2	–1.4	–1.0
Unemployment rate (difference)	WUMM	–0.0	–0.4	–0.9	–0.9	–0.7
	FRB-US	–0.0	–0.1	–0.4	–0.7	–0.7
Hourly nominal compensation growth (Q4 over Q4)	WUMM	–1.1	–0.8	–1.2	–0.1	–0.1
	FRB-US	–1.4	–1.3	–2.0	–0.4	–0.2

Source: Authors' calculations.

years. As a result, inflation remains about a percentage point below its baseline level in 1999, even though the benefits shock is gone. In the WUMM, nominal wage growth depends on anticipated nominal *wage* inflation instead of on anticipated *price* inflation, but the virtuous-circle mechanism is similar.

Regardless of whether the z_1 shock came from traumatized workers or from decelerating benefit costs, there remains the question of how long it continued to pull inflation down. As job prospects brightened in the tight labor markets of 1998 and 1999 and permanent layoffs declined to more normal levels, Americans workers should have overcome their trauma.[18] And benefit cost increases began to rise again in 1998. Moreover, any downward deflection of the path of benefits should ultimately have led to an upward deflection of the path of straight wages, as we have already noted. However, the expected effects of these wage-reducing events would have been more durable if labor's bargaining power had been permanently eroded. Furthermore, there were other factors holding price inflation down, factors to which we now turn.

Price Shocks during the Good Luck Period: 1996–98

Between 1996 and 1998, a series of favorable price shocks—negative z_2s—were reducing inflation below the rates that would have been predicted from the prevailing unemployment rate and past inflation history. In this chapter, we discuss three such shocks, leaving the surprising acceleration of productivity—surely the most important shock of the period—for separate treatment in Chapter 8. Simulations with the WUMM and FRB-US macroeconometric models described below suggest that these shocks are more than enough to explain why inflation was so well contained between 1996 and 1998.

The Dollar and Import Prices

A first favorable—albeit transitory—influence on inflation between 1995 and 1999 came from import prices. From the narrow standpoint of U.S. inflation, the sharp appreciation of the dollar from the spring of 1995 to the summer of 1998, coupled with a weak world economy, constituted a stroke of good fortune. As Figure 6.4 illustrates, the dollar rose sharply in real terms over these three years—at roughly a 4 percent average annual rate. With a short lag, the prices of nonoil imports mirrored this behavior, declining at a 4 percent annual rate during 1996–98 after rising at just under 1 percent per year during 1993–95. Because prices of imported goods are included in all indexes of consumer prices, falling import prices lowered these measures of inflation directly. They probably also constrained the pricing power of American businesses.

FIGURE 6.4. NONOIL IMPORT PRICES AND THE DOLLAR

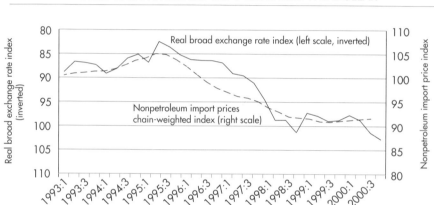

Source: Import prices from U.S. Department of Commerce, Bureau of Economic Analysis; exchange rate from Board of Governors of the Federal Reserve System.

With imports accounting for roughly 10 to 12 percent of the consumption basket, a simple back-of-the-envelope calculation suggests that the 18 percent appreciation of the dollar (on a trade-weighted basis) between 1995:2 and the end of 1998 should have lowered the level of consumer prices by about 2 percent. But this computation ignores all feedback and secondary effects. For a more serious assessment of the impact of the rising dollar on the U.S. economy during the good luck period, we again simulated both the WUMM and FRB-US macro models—asking what would have happened if the dollar had remained fixed in real terms after 1995:2.[19] The simulation again maintains the real federal funds rate at its actual baseline level. Table 6.3 shows the results and, unfortunately, the two models once again disagree—this time sharply.

In the WUMM model, the appreciation of the dollar has an extremely large negative impact on inflation, lowering CPI inflation by 0.6 percent during 1996, 1 percent during 1997, and a whopping 2.2 percent in 1998. In the absence of the appreciation, inflation during 1998 would have reached 3.7 percent (versus 1.5 percent in actuality), according to this model. The stunningly large impact, roughly triple what the elementary calculation suggests, comes largely from the sharp drop in real GDP (the growth-rate impacts shown in the table cumulate to a 5.5 percent level effect by the end of the simulation) and the accompanying rise in unemployment (2.5 percentage points). The FRB-US model produces inflation impacts that are similar qualitatively but much smaller quantitatively—owing largely to more muted effects on GDP and unemployment. According to this model, the biggest effect of the dollar appreciation on inflation reaches only –0.5 percent in 1998. Both models agree, however, that

TABLE 6.3. IMPACT OF THE REAL APPRECIATION
OF THE DOLLAR AFTER 1995:2
(REAL FEDERAL FUNDS RATE HELD AT BASELINE LEVEL)

DEVIATION FROM BASELINE	MODEL	1995:4	1996:4	1997:4	1998:4	1999:4
Real GDP growth (Q4 over Q4)	WUMM	–0.0	–0.2	–0.8	–2.2	–2.5
	FRB-US	–0.0	–0.2	–0.5	–1.0	–1.2
CPI inflation rate (Q4 over Q4)	WUMM	–0.1	–0.6	–1.0	–2.2	–2.0
	FRB-US	–0.0	–0.2	–0.3	–0.5	–0.3
Unemployment rate (difference)	WUMM	0.0	0.1	0.4	1.4	2.5
	FRB-US	0.0	0.0	0.1	0.5	1.0
Real broad exchange rate index (percent)	Both	3.3	5.3	14.6	17.9	18.5

Source: Authors' calculations.

the dollar's appreciation spared the Federal Reserve the need to raise the real federal funds rate to contain aggregate demand. Simulations of the two models (not shown) suggest that an increase in the real federal funds rate of 250 to 350 basis points would have been needed to hold unemployment to its historical path, if the dollar had not appreciated.

FALLING OIL PRICES

The effect of the strong dollar on inflation subsequently was reinforced by falling oil prices. Figure 6.5 shows that after rising during 1996, the price of petroleum fell roughly in half between the fourth quarter of 1996 and the first quarter of 1999. The decline in oil prices reduced energy costs, which directly lowered headline inflation relative to core measures. Lower energy costs may also have fed through into lower core inflation by holding down production costs.

In addition, the declining prices of both imports and energy may have led to more modest nominal wage increases, thereby reducing pressure on business costs and prices. Standard Phillips curve

FIGURE 6.5. DAILY PRICE OF WEST TEXAS INTERMEDIATE OIL

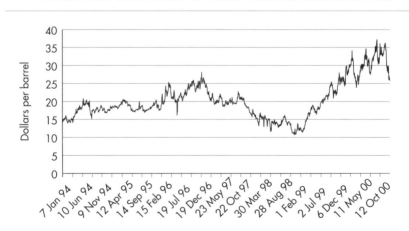

Source: Data taken from price quoted daily in the *Wall Street Journal.*

logic—embodied in equation (2) above—holds that tighter labor markets lead workers to demand (and businesses to provide) higher real wage increases. But falling import and energy prices may satisfy some of those demands without costing domestic producers anything. Consistent with this idea, the real consumption wage—defined as hourly compensation deflated by the CPI-U-RS—was essentially unchanged over the three years 1994–96, but then rose 2.7 percent per year during 1997 and 1998 as oil and import prices fell.

To study the consequences of the plunge in oil prices, we used the WUMM and FRB-US models to simulate what would have happened if the price of oil had remained at its 1996:1 level through the end of 1999 instead of fluctuating as it did—rising during 1996, falling during 1997 and 1998, and then rebounding during 1999.[20] (We again held the real funds rate constant.) Table 6.4 reports the results. In both models the oil shock lowers inflation slightly in 1997 and substantially (0.6 or 0.8 percent) in 1998. But note that the effects of the oil-price shock are estimated to have been substantially smaller than those of the other two shocks, even though it probably garnered the most public attention. Why? The bottom rows of Table 6.4 show the simple answer: the oil shock in 1996–99 was small compared to the OPEC shocks in the 1970s and early 1980s.

TABLE 6.4. IMPACT OF OIL PRICE FLUCTUATIONS AFTER 1996:1
(REAL FEDERAL FUNDS RATE HELD AT BASELINE LEVEL)

DEVIATION FROM BASELINE	MODEL	1996:4	1997:4	1998:4	1999:4
Real GDP growth (Q4 over Q4)	WUMM	−0.2	0.1	0.6	0.4
	FRB-US	0.0	0.1	0.0	−0.1
CPI inflation rate (Q4 over Q4)	WUMM	0.2	−0.1	−0.6	0.0
	FRB-US	0.3	−0.1	−0.8	0.0
Unemployment rate (difference)	WUMM	0.1	0.1	−0.1	−0.4
	FRB-US	0.0	0.0	−0.1	−0.2
Price of oil (percent difference)	WUMM	20.2	−4.9	−69.7	20.2
	FRB-US	21.4	1.5	−53.2	20.9

Source: Authors' calculations.

METHODOLOGICAL REVISIONS TO THE CPI

Measurement changes are not genuine economic shocks; they merely recalibrate the economy's thermometer. However, they did make macroeconomic performance look even better than it was between 1995 and 1999. Beginning in 1995, the Bureau of Labor Statistics (BLS) introduced a series of technical adjustments to the CPI that lowered measured inflation.[21] Although each individual change was small, the cumulative effect of these methodological changes was substantial: in total, they reduced measured CPI inflation by about 0.6 percent per annum by 1999.[22] Without these measurement changes, the reported CPI inflation rate would have been about 2.5 percent (rather than 1.9 percent) during 1999, and there would have been much less talk about the "miraculous" decline of inflation.

In adjusting the measurement system, the administration was not rigging the deck. Researchers had long believed that the CPI and other price indexes suffered from a variety of upward biases. Although bias in a price index is a rather esoteric subject, it began to captivate lawmakers when budget cutters (led by Senator Daniel Patrick Moynihan) focused on reducing the CPI as a source of budgetary savings. Since the CPI is used to compute cost-of-living adjustments in Social Security, other federal retirement programs, and the tax system, lower measured inflation would reduce federal outlays and boost tax receipts. In 1996, the Senate Finance Committee published the Boskin Commission report (named for its chairman, economist Michael Boskin), which estimated that the CPI inflation rate was biased upward by about 1.1 percentage points. The commission estimated that fixing this bias in 1997 would lower the federal deficit by $148 billion in 2006 and reduce the outstanding federal debt by $691 billion by that time.[23]

It is difficult to know whether the lower announced inflation rates affected economic behavior in any way. *Homo economicus* should not be deluded by bad data. But much of the observed decline in core CPI inflation from 1995 to 1999 was due to measurement changes rather than to genuine disinflation, and we doubt that many members of the public understood this.[24] Hence, we do not rule out the possibility that lower reported inflation was mistaken by at least some wage and price setters as lower true inflation, thereby leading to more modest wage settlements.

ASSESSING THE IMPACT OF WAGE-PRICE SHOCKS

Are the wage-price shocks discussed thus far sufficient to account for the favorable inflation/unemployment performance during the good luck period? We summarize the results of this chapter in Tables 6.5 and 6.6 (page 50). These tables show, for the FRB-US and WUMM models respectively, the combined impact of the wage-price

TABLE 6.5. ESTIMATED IMPACTS OF WAGE-PRICE SHOCKS
ON INFLATION AND UNEMPLOYMENT, FRB-US MODEL
(REAL FEDERAL FUNDS RATE HELD AT BASELINE LEVEL)

	1994	1995	1996	1997	1998	1999
Actual CPI inflation— Q4 over Q4	**2.6**	**2.7**	**3.1**	**1.9**	**1.5**	**2.6**
Difference without:						
Benefits shock	0.0	0.2	0.7	1.2	1.4	1.0
Real exchange rate appreciation	0.0	0.0	0.2	0.3	0.5	0.3
Oil price fluctuations after 1996:1	0.0	0.0	−0.3	0.1	0.8	0.0
Measurement changes	0.0	0.1	0.2	0.2	0.4	0.6
CPI inflation without "wage-price shocks"	**2.6**	**3.0**	**3.9**	**3.7**	**4.6**	**4.5**
Actual unemployment (Q4)	**5.6**	**5.6**	**5.3**	**4.7**	**4.4**	**4.1**
Difference without:						
Benefits shock	0.0	0.0	0.1	0.4	0.7	0.7
Real exchange rate appreciation	0.0	0.0	0.0	−0.1	−0.5	−1.0
Oil price fluctuations after 1996:1	0.0	0.0	0.0	0.0	0.1	0.2
Unemployment without "wage-price shocks"	**5.6**	**5.6**	**5.4**	**5.0**	**4.7**	**4.0**

Source: Authors' calculations.

TABLE 6.6. ESTIMATED IMPACTS OF WAGE-PRICE SHOCKS
ON INFLATION AND UNEMPLOYMENT, WUMM MODEL
(REAL FEDERAL FUNDS RATE HELD AT BASELINE LEVEL)

	1994	1995	1996	1997	1998	1999
Actual CPI inflation—Q4 over Q4	**2.6**	**2.7**	**3.1**	**1.9**	**1.5**	**2.6**
Difference without:						
Benefits shock	0.0	0.8	1.3	1.5	0.7	0.3
Real exchange rate appreciation	0.0	0.1	0.6	1.0	2.2	2.0
Oil price fluctuations after 1996:1	0.0	0.0	−0.2	0.1	0.6	0.0
Measurement changes	0.0	0.1	0.2	0.2	0.4	0.6
CPI inflation without "wage-price shocks"	**2.6**	**3.7**	**5.0**	**4.7**	**5.4**	**5.5**
Actual unemployment (Q4 level)	**5.6**	**5.6**	**5.3**	**4.7**	**4.4**	**4.1**
Difference without:						
Benefits shock	0.0	0.0	0.4	0.9	0.9	0.7
Real exchange rate appreciation	0.0	0.0	−0.1	−0.4	−1.4	−2.5
Oil price fluctuations after 1996:1	0.0	0.0	−0.1	−0.1	0.1	0.4
Unemployment without "wage-price shocks"	**5.6**	**5.6**	**5.5**	**5.1**	**4.0**	**2.7**

Source: Authors' calculations.

shocks on the paths of unemployment and inflation between 1994 and 1999. The underlying simulations all assume that the Federal Reserve would have held the real federal funds rate at its actual historical level in the absence of the shocks.

According to the FRB-US model, the joint impact of the benefits, exchange rate, oil, and measurement shocks was to lower unemployment slightly and inflation substantially by 1997–99. Remember, it was the low inflation rates of the years 1997 and 1998 that stood out in Figure 6.1 (page 38). Absent the shocks, the model says that inflation would have accelerated by two percentage points between 1994 and 1998, reaching 4.6 percent in 1998. According to the WUMM model, the shocks had little net effect on the *average* unemployment rate in 1997 and 1998, but lowered inflation substantially in every year from 1995 through 1999. Absent the shocks, inflation would have accelerated from 2.6 percent in 1994 to 5.4 percent in 1998, rather than falling to 1.5 percent.

So, do the four supply shocks listed in Tables 6.5 and 6.6 explain what actually happened to inflation and unemployment between, say, late 1994 and late 1998? Both models say yes. Each estimates that, with the real federal funds rate held constant, the supply shocks barely changed the average unemployment rate over the four-year period, but reduced the 1998 inflation rate by 3.1 percentage points (in FRB-US) or 3.9 percentage points (in WUMM). These are very sizable impacts. By comparison, the differences across the two models seem small.

To put these estimates into perspective, suppose you believed that the NAIRU was about 6 percent, as many economists (and the Fed) did in 1994. Then, from the end of 1994 through the end of 1998, the economy enjoyed 3.6 "point years" of unemployment below NAIRU. According to a popular Phillips curve rule of thumb, that should have pushed inflation up by about 1.8 percentage points. Instead, inflation actually fell by 1.1 percentage points. The discrepancy—an inflation "surprise" of 2.9 percentage points—is very close to the FRB-US estimate of the disinflationary impact of the supply shocks (but less than the WUMM's). In brief, according to the models, the four supply shocks either explain (FRB-US) or over-explain (WUMM) the drop in inflation. Without those shocks, inflation would have risen to about 5 percent by the end of 1998, according to the models.

THE FED PONDERS THE SUPPLY SHOCKS

As these favorable price developments nudged inflation downward, the Fed was pleased, if somewhat surprised. Although aware that favorable supply shocks could permit very low unemployment to coexist with stable or even falling inflation for a time, the FOMC retained a nagging fear: maybe the lucky streak was about to end, and inflation would rise again. Members were justifiably concerned that the disinflationary benefits of the strong dollar and lower oil prices were only temporary, and they worried that employee benefits would rise more rapidly once workers had been shifted into managed care and the "trauma" of a weak labor market had disappeared from memories. Federal Reserve Governor Laurence Meyer began calling the period one of "temporary bliss."[25]

But what about the possibility that the superior inflation performance reflected permanent, or at least very long-lasting, "bliss"? It was during this good luck period (1996–98) that Greenspan, the alleged inflation hawk, revealed himself to be the committee's most ardent advocate of New Economy thinking: that productivity gains and worker insecurity were holding down both compensation and inflation—and might do so for a significant period of time. This view rationalized a strategy of continued forbearance in the face of extraordinarily low unemployment, and Greenspan led his sometimes-balky committee to do precisely that. The Fed raised interest rates only once, and then by a mere 25 basis points (in March 1997).

Many outside observers, and some within the FOMC, thought the dovish Greenspan was "pushing the envelope." During 1996 and 1997, one or two members occasionally dissented in favor of tightening, and the minutes indicate pretty clearly that others held similar views but did not oppose the chairman. However, given increased uncertainty about structural shifts—and the fact that inflation was falling, not rising—Greenspan was able to persuade his committee not to attack inflation "preemptively" but rather to wait to shoot until they could see the whites of rising inflation's eyes. And that, of course, never happened.

In a series of speeches, Meyer articulated an intellectual justification for the Fed's change in strategy—which amounted to abandoning the former policy of preemption in favor of forbearance.[26] The essence of the case was pretty simple. The preemptive strategy relied on some (albeit imperfect) ability to forecast inflation. With extreme uncertainty over the NAIRU and other aspects of the Phillips curve, one could argue that it no longer made sense to act on the basis of forecasts, for the risks of making a major policy error were simply too great. Instead, Meyer suggested, the Fed should wait until it saw clear evidence of rising inflation. But then, he added, since the Fed would be "behind the curve" when it finally acted, it should raise rates aggressively.

Regardless of this intellectual debate, and of disagreements within the FOMC, no one should think the FOMC's "experiment" of allowing unemployment to drift down to thirty-year lows was a deliberate policy decision. It was largely inadvertent. For most of the 1996–98 period, the Fed was consistently surprised by the strength of aggregate demand and the drop in the unemployment rate, just like most forecasters. We find it impossible to believe that the committee would have deliberately chosen to push unemployment below 5 percent, much less all the way down to 4 percent. Indeed, a substantial number of FOMC members shared the typical staff forecasts that higher inflation was likely if unemployment remained at prevailing rates. Like the Blue Chip consensus, the Fed's staff forecasts typically saw a growth slowdown just around the corner. But the slowdown never materialized. On the other hand, as growth constantly outstripped forecasts and unemployment fell, the Fed made no effort to push unemployment back toward any preconceived notion of the NAIRU. That was its real experiment.

THE ROLE OF DEMAND SHOCKS IN THE GOOD LUCK PERIOD

The unexpected strength of demand during the 1996–98 period arguably derived from the gravity-defying stock market, which stoked demand and drove the personal saving rate down.[27] The stock market was thus a topic that preoccupied the Fed. At a consultants' meeting in November 1996, the Board of Governors heard opinions about the stock market from a group of academic economists and Wall Street analysts—including stock market bears Robert Shiller and John Campbell. In a speech the next month, Greenspan added a phrase to the English language when he famously ruminated: "But how do we know when irrational exuberance has unduly escalated asset values, which then become subject to unexpected and prolonged contractions. . . ? And how do we factor that assessment into monetary policy?"[28] Such "thinking out loud"—said to be the first time a Fed chairman had discussed stock market valuations in thirty years—touched off a short but furious flurry of selling.

The (consistently incorrect) belief that stock market gains would cease or be reversed was one justification for forecasting a slowdown. But the stock market was not the only phenomenon that consistently surprised forecasters on the upside; so did business investment. The behavior of both stock prices and capital formation were consistent with the argument that an unrecognized productivity shock was driving both aggregate supply and aggregate demand during the second half of the 1990s.

Nonetheless, the Fed seemed poised to tighten further in the summer of 1997 when a series of events in Asia cast doubt on the durability of the U.S. expansion. In July, the Thai baht succumbed to speculative attack and was devalued. The minutes of the August FOMC meeting contain no reference to the Thai situation, which may seem surprising. But few observers initially imagined that this episode would mark the beginning of a global financial crisis that would, in some sense, continue to rumble around the world for more than a year.

By September, however, the crisis had spread to Indonesia, Malaysia, and the Philippines; Singapore and Taiwan had floated their currencies; and contagion was also affecting Hong Kong. The deteriorating international situation altered the FOMC's calculus profoundly. The Fed recognized that the Asian shock would both reduce inflationary pressures and cut U.S. exports. Furthermore, there was a danger that the financial crisis might spread—thereby creating more downside risk. The crisis thus created a rationale to continue the policy of forbearance despite rapid growth in already tight labor markets.[29]

Continued forbearance may also have been motivated by a concern that further tightening would intensify financial pressures on the crisis countries and their major trading partners, thereby exacerbating a rapidly deteriorating international financial situation. Treasury Secretary Robert Rubin repeatedly urged all G-7 countries to pursue expansionary policies, including monetary policy, to mitigate the growing downside risks to the global economy. A tightening of U.S. monetary policy, regardless of its domestic logic, would have undermined this broader economic agenda. The May 1998 FOMC minutes justify the committee's inaction as due, in part, to "the possibility that even a modest tightening action could have outsized effects on the already very sensitive financial markets in Asia." Since the Fed's statutory mandate provides no authority for policy actions undertaken mainly to foster improved economic conditions abroad, the committee rationalized its decision by stating that, "The resulting unsettlement could have substantial adverse repercussions on U.S. financial markets and, over time, on the U.S. economy."

By the spring of 1998, the Fed again had its finger on the interest rate trigger. But, once again, it did not fire. Just a few months later, Russia's devaluation and default in August 1998 dramatically changed the outlook, the risks, and the Fed's policy. Between September and November 1998, the Fed actually eased by 75 basis points in response to the worsening international financial crisis. The first cut came in the wake of the Russian default, amidst evidence of sharply higher risk spreads, more cautious lending by U.S. banks, a decline in equity prices, and a distinct downgrading of prospects for global growth. The second cut came as a rare intrameeting move following the collapse of the huge (and poorly hedged) hedge fund Long Term Capital Management, a shock that resulted in a temporary but frightening drying up of liquidity in most financial markets and an alarming spike in risk spreads.[30]

Thus the Fed might well have tightened monetary policy both in 1997 and again in 1998 were it not for surprising, and somewhat ominous, events originating abroad. The period of forbearance was thus extended unnaturally.

7.

THE END OF FORBEARANCE

B y the start of 1999, most of the supply shocks that had held inflation down during the good luck period had dissipated or even
reversed. Nonetheless, both unemployment and core inflation continued to inch downward. By June, however, the policy of forbearance
had finally taxed the Fed's patience, and the FOMC embarked on a
tightening cycle (depicted earlier in Figure 5.2, page 29) that would
take the Fed funds rate from 4.75 percent in June 1999 to 6.5 percent
by May 2000. For the second time during the 1990s, the Fed would
attempt a soft landing.

Given the inherently temporary nature of at least some of the
favorable supply shocks, economists were hardly surprised when
these factors began to ebb or reverse:

- The dollar peaked against a broad basket of currencies in August
  1998, then fluctuated in a relatively narrow band near that level
  through 1999. This brought the inflation bonus from falling
  import prices first to a crawl and then to a halt.

- Energy prices reversed course during 1999. With OPEC production cuts and recovery in the global economy, the price of oil
  soared 93 percent during 1999, fully retracing its downward
  steps and then rising even further in 2000. Table 6.1 (page 36)
  shows that surging energy prices pushed headline inflation measures up by more than a full percentage point during 1999, even
  though core inflation was stable or falling.

- Forecasters had long feared that employer costs for health benefits would escalate again once the one-time gains from switching
  workers from fee-for-service to managed care were exhausted.
  And they did. By the end of 1999, benefit costs were increasing
  sharply.

- The pace of price declines for computers and semiconductors,
  which had soared to near 30 percent per annum during the good
  luck period, slowed to a "mere" 21 percent on a quality-adjusted
  basis during 1999. (See Chapter 8.)

Despite all this, core consumer inflation dropped in 1999. Why
did inflation remain low during 1999 despite such reversals of good
fortune? Perhaps the most plausible answer credits accelerating productivity growth with keeping unit labor costs in check. Between
1996 and 1999, productivity growth averaged 2.5 percent per year—
almost a percentage point higher than its average from 1991 to 1995.
But, importantly, productivity was actually accelerating during this
period, reaching a stunning 4.1 percent annual rate during 1999. The
consequence was that unit labor costs rose at only a paltry 0.7 percent
pace that year.[1] At the end of the day, the acceleration in productivity proved to be a more important influence on inflation than the
disappearance of the favorable supply shocks. Though still too new to
be fully understood, this phenomenon merits detailed consideration.

8.

PRODUCTIVITY GROWTH AND COMPUTER PRICES

As late as 1998, advocates of the New Economy view—that computers and information technology were transforming American businesses and boosting productivity growth—could point to little in the way of hard data to make their case. Productivity growth had risen somewhat, but normal statistical tests attributed this rise to the cyclical upturn; there was no real evidence of any change in the underlying trend.[1] Yet stories proliferated of how the computer and the Internet were "changing everything." In brief, "Solow's paradox" was in full flower: the computer could be seen everywhere except in the productivity statistics.[2]

Still, a number of people entertained a tantalizing thought: suppose that, despite the official data, productivity really was surging. That could explain why investment was so strong, why corporate earnings were growing so rapidly, and why stock market valuations were skyrocketing. A rising statistical discrepancy in the national accounts, showing that incomes were growing notably faster than production (which is impossible), also suggested that productivity growth might be higher than recognized by the official (product side) measure. Alan Greenspan was a leading advocate of this more optimistic view.

With the benefit of hindsight and after several data revisions, it now appears that the anecdotes were running well ahead of the data: productivity growth was about a full percentage point higher in the years 1996–99 than during the earlier 1991–95 period. Statistical tests for a change in trend productivity growth clearly point to a break in late 1995 or early 1996 and Figure 8.1 indicates why. It gives a distinct visual impression of an acceleration in productivity beginning sometime around the end of 1995. But this was less obvious in real time.

FIGURE 8.1. FOUR-YEAR AVERAGE GROWTH OF PRODUCTIVITY IN NONFARM BUSINESS, 1963–2000

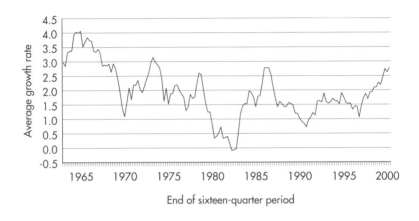

End of sixteen-quarter period

Source: U.S. Department of Labor, Bureau of Labor Statistics.

A series of simple regressions illustrates just how quickly the statistical story changed. Using quarterly data on hours and output in the nonfarm business sector, we estimated the following simple model to separate the trend and cyclical components of productivity growth:

$$(4)\ h_t = constant + a_1 y_t + a_2 y_{t-1} + b_1 h_{t-1} + b_2 h_{t-2} + time\ trends + error$$

where h is the log of hours of work and y is the log of output. Productivity is therefore $y - h$. The constraint (imposed in estimation) that $a_1 + a_2 + b_1 + b_2 = 1$ makes hours proportional to output in the long run, thus guaranteeing that any output effect on productivity is transitory. That is how we distinguish cycle from trend. Dummy variables for different time periods then pick up any breaks in the underlying trend, and the regressions we ran estimate three distinct time trends in order to test for two such structural breaks: one beginning in 1973:3 (the slowdown), and another beginning in 1995:4 (the speedup).

Table 8.1 summarizes the results of a series of regressions, each starting in 1959:3 but ending at different points. Since none of the other coefficients change much as we extend the sample, the table reports only the estimated break in the productivity trend at 1995:4 and its t-ratio.

TABLE 8.1. REGRESSION ESTIMATES OF EQUATION (4)
WITH DIFFERENT ENDPOINTS

ENDPOINT	ESTIMATED CHANGE IN TREND (%)	t-RATIO
1996:4	+0.82	.52
1997:1	+0.58	.46
1997:2	+0.71	.70
1997:3	+1.06	1.24
1997:4	+0.96	1.30
1998:1	+0.98	1.52
1998:2	+1.11	1.95
1998:3	+1.10	2.14
1998:4	+0.99	2.12
1999:1	+1.11	2.62
1999:2	+1.02	2.60
1999:3	+1.07	2.94
1999:4	+1.18	3.44
2000:1	+1.22	3.75
2000:2	+1.39	4.40
2000:3	+1.51	4.87
2000:4	+1.61	5.26

Source: Authors' calculations.

It is clear that, through early 1998, there was no substantial statistical evidence that the productivity trend had increased—even though the point estimate suggested roughly a one-percentage-point rise relative to the trend that prevailed from 1973 to 1995. (The highest t-ratio registered through 1998:1 is only 1.52, corresponding to a p-value of 0.13.) But the picture begins to change rapidly after that. By the time the third quarter of 1998 is added to the sample, the point estimate of the increase in trend productivity starting in 1995:4 is still around one percentage point, but its t-ratio has jumped to 2.14 (p-value = .03). By the time 1999:4 is included, the t-ratio reaches 3.44 (p = .0007) and the point estimate of the trend break is about 1.2 percentage points. In sum, it was not until mid to late 1998 that the data finally caught up with the anecdotes and verified that productivity had indeed accelerated.

What caused the surge in productivity growth? Technological improvements in the production of computers and semiconductors probably account for the lion's share, both directly and indirectly. First, impressive gains in computer-industry productivity were a direct and major contributor to overall, economywide productivity growth. Second, the falling prices of computers and software led to increased investment in and use of computers throughout the economy—so-called capital deepening. Third, and perhaps most controversially, improvements in information technology (IT) boosted productivity in the sectors of the economy that use computers intensively.

Figure 8.2 depicts the truly remarkable behavior of computer prices. After falling at an average annual rate of around 14 percent in nominal terms over the fifteen-year-period from 1980 to 1995, computer deflation soared into the 25 to 30 percent range during the following three years. These sharp price declines reflected the stunning pickup in total factor productivity (TFP) growth in this sector, as Moore's Law was violated.[3] Although computers and semiconductors account for a mere 1.5 percent of nonfarm business output, estimates by Fed economists Stephen Oliner and Daniel Sichel suggest that the speedup in TFP growth in computers was sufficient to raise aggregate TFP by about 0.35 percentage point during the second half of the 1990s.[4] And they estimate about an equal contribution from TFP in the rest of the nonfarm business sector. Northwestern University economist Robert Gordon estimates about the same effect in the computer industry, but no speedup in TFP growth in the rest of the economy.[5]

FIGURE 8.2. CHANGES IN COMPUTER PRICES[a]

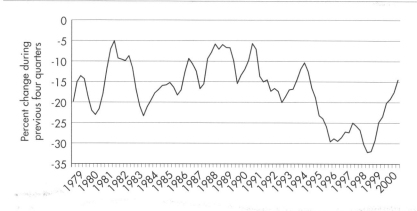

[a] Chain-type price index for final computer sales—four-quarter trailing change.
Source: U.S. Department of Commerce, Bureau of Economic Analysis.

The key reason for the difference is that Gordon makes a cyclical adjustment while Oliner and Sichel do not.

Beyond this direct effect, rapid price reductions for computers and information technology equipment raised productivity growth via an important indirect channel that is often ignored: lower equipment prices helped trigger an investment boom.[6] By 1999, real investment as a share of GDP stood at its highest level in the postwar period, and this flood of new investment was concentrated in high-tech equipment and software. Oliner and Sichel estimate that capital deepening raised the productivity growth rate during 1996–99 by 0.5 percent, with almost the entire increase concentrated in computers and information technology equipment.[7] In retrospect, some of this high-tech investment may have been part of the great speculative bubble of 1998–2000; but few observers were saying so at the time.

A pickup in productivity growth is, of course, extremely good news for long-run living standards, especially following decades of disappointingly slow real wage growth. From the standpoint of unemployment and inflation, however, the key question is whether and how such productivity improvement affected the Phillips curve.

One plausible story is that the productivity shock reduced the "short-run NAIRU," the unemployment rate consistent with stable inflation, at least for a time, by holding down increases in unit labor costs despite gains in nominal wages. But wait. Shouldn't faster productivity growth translate one-to-one into faster wage settlements, as in equation (1) above, leaving no net change in the path of unit labor costs? After all, economists normally assume that this is so—that is, that $x^w = x^f$. However, the speedup in productivity growth may have gone *unrecognized,* at least for a time. Alternatively, the real wage aspirations of workers, embodied in the norms that condition wage bargaining (x^w), might have been depressed after two decades of real wage stagnation and therefore slow to react to the new reality of faster productivity growth.[8] These two hypotheses sound, and in some sense are, different. But they carry almost identical implications for observable variables. In either case, wage settlements should come in "too low" relative to the now-faster productivity gains.

The failure of wage settlements to increase in tandem with productivity would, in turn, have two principal effects. First, with labor now suddenly cheaper relative to its productivity, firms would naturally want to do more hiring. So unemployment would fall. Second, the path of unit labor costs would be deflected downward, easing any pressures on firms to raise prices. So inflation would also fall. In brief, a surprise increase in the productivity growth rate should reduce unemployment and inflation at the same time, which is precisely what happened in the late 1990s.[9] Indeed, this story simply takes a widely accepted explanation for the stagflation of the 1970s and runs it in reverse. In the 1970s, an unrecognized productivity *slowdown* led to "excessive" wage settlements, more inflation, and less employment. In the 1990s, an unrecognized productivity *speedup* had precisely the opposite effects.

To quantify the effects of the productivity improvement, we again employed our two macroeconometric models with the real federal funds rate held at baseline levels. But since the two models treat trend productivity differently, the two simulations had to be done in rather different ways. We began with a simulation using the FRB-US model, which zeroed out the entire speedup in productivity growth in the nonfarm business sector that began in 1994.[10]

The results, displayed in Table 8.2, show that productivity growth raises aggregate demand by even more than it raises aggregate supply in the FRB-US model. Wealth effects boost consumption, and faster GDP growth produces notable accelerator effects on housing,

TABLE 8.2. IMPACT OF FASTER TREND PRODUCTIVITY AFTER 1993
(REAL FEDERAL FUNDS RATE HELD AT BASELINE LEVEL)

DEVIATION FROM BASELINE	MODEL	1996:4	1997:4	1998:4	1999:4
Real GDP growth (Q4 over Q4)	WUMM	0.9	1.2	0.9	1.1
	FRB-US	1.1	1.3	1.7	1.6
CPI inflation rate (Q4 over Q4)	WUMM	−0.9	−1.1	−1.4	−1.7
	FRB-US	−0.3	−0.2	−0.0	0.3
Unemployment rate (difference)	WUMM	0.1	0.0	0.1	0.0
	FRB-US	−0.4	−0.7	−1.0	−1.3
Trend labor productivity in nonfarm business (percent difference)	Both	1.5	2.5	3.9	5.4
Growth rate of trend labor productivity in nonfarm business, Q4 over Q4 (difference)	Both	0.7	1.0	1.3	1.5

Source: Authors' calculations.

consumer durables, and business investment. As a result, while the
level of trend labor productivity in the nonfarm business sector is up
5.4 percent, raising *potential* real GDP about 4.3 percent by the end
of the simulation, the growth rate of *actual* real GDP rises enough
(about 1.15 percentage points per annum for six years) to leave the
level of GDP 6.8 percent higher. So the unemployment rate actually
winds up 1.3 percentage points lower by the end of 1999. Although
inflation is initially depressed a bit by the productivity surge, the
lower unemployment causes it to creep up over time—ending up
slightly above the baseline level in 1999.[11]

To create a comparable simulation with the WUMM model, we
began by asking what would have happened in the absence of more
rapid TFP growth in computers. So we started by holding the relative
price decline for computers to its 1993 pace (which was −7.5 percent
per annum in the model), thus disallowing the apparent acceleration in
technological change after 1994.[12] But that cancelled out only part of

the post-1994 surge in productivity, so we also reduced TFP outside the computer sector by just enough to replicate the productivity decline in the nonfarm business sector simulated in the FRB-US model.

In the WUMM simulation, the aggregate supply and aggregate demand impacts of the productivity shock roughly cancel one another out, leaving the unemployment rate essentially unchanged under a monetary policy that holds the real federal funds rate constant. According to the WUMM, the productivity shock added roughly a percentage point a year to the growth rate of real GDP while reducing the inflation rate a remarkable 1.7 percent by 1999. Both models agree that accelerating productivity lowered inflation after 1995, but the WUMM model estimates a far larger impact.

A natural question to ask is why the two models yield such different estimates of the disinflationary impact of the productivity surge. One reason is that the dividend resulting from the productivity shock is disproportionately devoted to lower *unemployment* in the FRB-US model versus lower *inflation* in the WUMM. In addition, the two models differ in their treatment of wage-price dynamics. The FRB-US model incorporates differential lags in the responses of wages and prices to productivity shocks, which is reminiscent of our canonical Phillips curve model—equations (1), (2), and (3), above—with $x^w < x^f$. Following a one-time jump in productivity growth, price expectations take about a year to adjust, but wage expectations take longer—about three years. So it is as if $x^f > x^w$ for about two years.

In the WUMM model, this asymmetry is far more pronounced and lasts substantially longer. The response of nominal wage growth to productivity shocks is especially sluggish because, in contrast to equation (1), the WUMM model assumes that past nominal wage growth, not expected inflation nor perceived productivity growth, influences wage bargains. Thus, the two models agree that the productivity shock had a profound impact on economic performance during the second half of the 1990s, but they disagree about the magnitude and duration of the "disinflation" resulting from the shock.[13]

Does the hypothesis that productivity growth influenced the Phillips curve tradeoff really explain what happened? Absent hard data on either perceived productivity gains or wage aspirations, it is impossible to know for sure. But notice one critical implication of the misperception view: The extraordinary combination of low inflation and low unemployment that we have enjoyed in recent years should be mostly transitory. As workers come to realize that productivity is rising faster, they will demand more generous real wage increases. As firms begin to grant these wage increases, their costs will rise. On this view, the short-run Phillips curve tradeoff should return to normal as perceptions catch up to reality. In theory, and in both of the simulation models, the "bliss" is only temporary.

More or less the same story holds if lagging real wage aspirations lie behind the shifting Phillips curve. However, the effect would be expected to last longer if the underlying phenomenon was a durable weakening of labor's bargaining position. In that case, the favorable shift in the Phillips curve might be expected to endure.

THE IMPACT OF SUPPLY SHOCKS: A SUMMARY

The United States enjoyed a large dose of good luck during the second half of the 1990s: a productivity surge, slower growth in fringe benefits, a rising dollar, falling oil prices, and a series of measurement changes that lowered inflation. How different would the U.S. experience after 1994 have been if none of these favorable shocks had occurred (but the Federal Reserve had nevertheless held the real federal funds rate to its actual historical path)? Table 8.3 summarizes the answers given by our two macroeconometric models; it

TABLE 8.3. THE IMPACT OF SUPPLY SHOCKS ON INFLATION AND UNEMPLOYMENT AFTER 1994
(REAL FEDERAL FUNDS RATE HELD AT BASELINE LEVEL)

	MODEL	1993	1994	1995	1996	1997	1998	1999
Actual CPI inflation (Q4 over Q4)		2.7	2.6	2.7	3.1	1.9	1.5	2.6
CPI inflation without any shocks	WUMM	2.7	2.8	4.4	5.9	5.8	6.8	7.2
	FRB-US	2.7	2.6	3.3	4.2	3.9	4.6	4.2
Actual unemployment (Q4)		6.6	5.6	5.6	5.3	4.7	4.4	4.1
Unemployment without any shocks	WUMM	6.6	5.4	5.4	5.4	5.1	3.9	2.7
	FRB-US	6.6	5.6	5.8	5.8	5.9	5.7	5.3

Source: Authors' calculations.

essentially adds the impacts of the productivity shock to the results shown earlier in Tables 6.5 and 6.6 (pages 49 and 50).

According to the FRB-US model, unemployment would have stayed in the 5 to 6 percent range—essentially remaining near 1994 levels. And yet inflation would have drifted up from just above 2.5 percent to over 4 percent. In a word, there would have been no macroeconomic miracle. The WUMM's answer is different. According to this simulation, the Fed's actual monetary policy would have been so easy under the circumstances that unemployment would eventually have fallen below 3 percent. Not surprisingly, that would have driven inflation much higher—to above 7 percent by the end of the decade. These calculations suggest that, once the improvement in trend productivity is taken into account, all the supply shocks together over-explain the excellent inflation performance slightly after 1994. The favorable impact of the shocks on the Phillips curve is so large, according to the two models, that we are left wondering why inflation was not even lower.

9.

MONETARY POLICY IN
1999 AND AFTER

About midway through 1999, the Fed abandoned its policy of
watchful waiting and embarked on a campaign to slow the growth
of aggregate demand down to that of aggregate supply, thereby preventing labor markets from tightening even further. By the time this
decision was taken, the unemployment rate had fallen to 4.2 percent,
the favorable supply shocks had ended or were reversing, and the
global economy was clearly on the mend. That might seem like sufficient reason to justify rate hikes. But the FOMC still saw no evidence of rising inflation. Productivity was rising sharply, and the Fed
believed that the prolonged period of low inflation had reduced inflationary expectations and therefore compensation growth. In view of
all this, why tighten?

What finally motivated the switch to a tightening stance was the
recognition that aggregate demand growth was unlikely to diminish
toward the (now faster) estimated trend in potential output unless
interest rates were raised. The FOMC had expected and waited for
such a slowdown for a long time. The minutes suggest that members
had, in effect, agreed to disagree over whether structural changes had
reduced the NAIRU permanently. Some were obviously skeptical that
an unemployment rate as low as 4.2 percent could be maintained for
long without rising inflation—even if productivity growth was still on
the rise. Others, presumably including Alan Greenspan, were less
enamored of the NAIRU approach, more willing to believe that wage-
setting behavior had changed, and more open to the possibility that
productivity might accelerate even more. But even the Fed's doves

agreed that inflation risks would rise if the labor market were allowed to tighten further. The strategy of raising the federal funds rate by enough to slow aggregate demand growth to trend—thus holding the unemployment rate constant—was a kind of middle ground that reduced, but did not eliminate, the risk of rising inflation.

Another factor pushing the funds rate up was the Fed's belief that the economy's demand for both consumer and investment goods had increased, raising the equilibrium real funds rate. In explaining the FOMC's decisions, Greenspan argued that the acceleration in productivity had boosted the equilibrium real rate. Faster productivity growth not only raised the growth rate of potential GDP, he said, but also raised the growth rate of actual GDP—as was the case in the FRB-US simulation in Table 8.2 (page 65). One channel works through investment: when falling computer prices and technological innovation raise the anticipated real rate of return, the investment function shifts out. The other channel works through consumption: wealth effects from the soaring stock market spur consumption growth in excess of income growth.[1]

The surge in stock prices, in turn, arguably reflected higher anticipated future earnings, another presumed result of the productivity boom. In addition, many economists argued that there were good reasons to think that the equity premium might have declined.[2] However, many observers—both economists and noneconomists—continued to wonder whether the behavior of stock prices could really be justified by the improved "fundamentals," favorable as they were. If soaring equity prices reflected "irrational exuberance" as much as (or more than) any rational assessment of likely future earnings streams, the economy was riding in part on an artificial high. This possibility—which by late 2000 certainly looked like a strong probability—clearly worried the Fed in 1998 and 1999.

Of course, one channel by which a higher federal funds rate works to contain aggregate demand is by reining in the stock market. The Fed thus had a difficult public relations task on its hands: explaining that monetary policy was not targeting the stock market, but that it nonetheless had to take the impact of stock prices on the economy into account.

The notion that the productivity shock contributed to robust domestic demand growth is interesting and empirically plausible. But it was not the only rationale for tighter monetary policy. Broader measures of financial conditions, which accounted inter alia for the booming stock market, suggested that financial markets were not feeling much of a pinch. And, most important, there was simply too little evidence that demand was slowing down—suggesting to the Fed that a higher real funds rate was warranted. So rates headed up.

10.

THE AMAZING, VANISHING BUDGET DEFICIT

While the Federal Reserve was first practicing forbearance and then tightening, the government's fiscal position was changing at breathtaking speed. We argued earlier that the 1993 budget agreement was a turning point for fiscal policy. But it did not complete the job of deficit reduction, and it certainly did not end the partisan rancor. The years 1995 and 1996 were marked by particularly contentious budget battles between the White House and the Republican-controlled Congress—leading to two government shutdowns, a threat by Congress to force the Treasury to default on the national debt, and the frequent operation of the U.S. government under a series of stopgap spending bills (so-called continuing resolutions). In 1995, the House passed and the Senate nearly passed a Balanced Budget Amendment to the Constitution, a centerpiece of Speaker Newt Gingrich's "Contract with America."

The budget deficit fared far better than the politics, however, declining much faster than the administration had claimed in 1993: from $290 billion in 1992 to just $108 billion in 1996. Nonetheless, as Bill Clinton began his second term, the CBO was projecting that the deficit would again rise to $188 billion by 2002. Furthermore, some critics attributed the falling deficit to the strong economy. That was mostly incorrect. While a portion (about 25 percent) of the improvement in the budget was indeed cyclical, the lion's share reflected a better structural balance.[1]

The 1993 agreement had set strict caps on discretionary spending through 1998, and those caps effectively constrained appropriations.

But the caps were about to expire, and Congress was once again threatening to pass a Balanced Budget Amendment. Eager to finish the job and to claim fiscal victory, the president made negotiating a new agreement to achieve a balanced budget by 2002 his highest post-election priority.

As political negotiations opened in early 1997, it appeared that the task of balancing the budget by 2002, though feasible, was going to be painful. Tax hikes were off the table; indeed, both parties were now on record as favoring a variety of tax cuts. And discretionary spending had already declined roughly 11 percent in real terms between 1992 and 1997. Further progress would be difficult because the entire cut had, to that point, come from the defense budget. Because the scope for additional cuts in defense was deemed limited, contentious cuts in civilian spending or in entitlements such as Medicare, Medicaid, and Social Security would be needed—not to mention battles over the size and nature of any tax cuts. But despite these formidable obstacles, the White House and Congress did manage to reach an agreement to balance the budget, enabling the president to declare victory in the war against deficits.

As politics, the 1997 budget agreement was a notable achievement. It included significant cuts in entitlements, particularly in Medicare—a sign of its "seriousness"—and it extended the budget enforcement mechanisms that had effectively restrained discretionary spending since 1990. Newly negotiated spending caps promised (if implausibly) to hold discretionary spending approximately constant in nominal terms between 1998 and 2002. However, the agreement conveniently postponed the difficult decisions of how the corresponding real cuts—roughly 10 percent over four years—would be achieved. In the event, Congress and the president found it impossible to live within the caps and busted them with emergency appropriations and other budgetary devices in fiscal years 1999, 2000, and 2001. Nonetheless, the caps set in the 1997 agreement continued to shape budget debates by determining the baseline for discussion.

From a macroeconomic perspective, however, the 1997 budget agreement did not amount to much. In fact, with its small tax cuts and more generous cap on discretionary spending for 1998, the 1997 agreement actually increased the deficit by about $21 billion in its first year.[2] Naturally, it did not provoke any noticeable reaction either in the financial markets or from the Federal Reserve.

But a minor budget miracle happened. By the beginning of 1998, the fiscal outlook had improved so dramatically that President Clinton could propose using the emerging surpluses to tackle the massive fiscal problems implied by an aging population—as he put it, to "save Social Security first." A year and a half later, the administration projected that the entire publicly held federal debt would be paid off by 2015,[3] a time frame that was subsequently shortened. Either of these ideas would have been greeted with howls of incredulity only a few years earlier. A program that was advertised to produce budget balance by 2002 had somehow produced a surplus by 1998.

The emergence of budget surpluses raises several interesting questions. The first is simply how they materialized. Figure 10.1 depicts the CBO's projections of the federal budget for fiscal years 1997–2002, made at roughly six-month intervals from January 1997 to July 2000.[4] It shows a dramatic sequence of upward revisions. For example, between January 1997 and August 2000, the CBO's forecast of the fiscal year 2000 balance rose from a $171 billion deficit to a $232 billion surplus—a swing of $403 billion. The CBO's forecast of the fiscal year 2002 surplus rose even more: by $593 billion. These are staggering revisions.

FIGURE 10.1. THE EVOLUTION OF CBO SURPLUS
PROJECTIONS FOR FISCAL YEARS 1997–2002

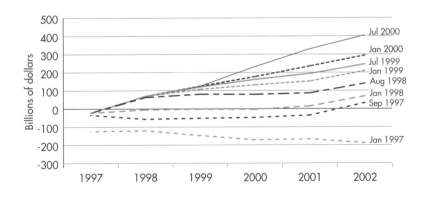

Source: Congressional Budget Office.

Figure 10.2 breaks these upward revisions into three sources: legislative or policy changes, changes in economic forecasts, and "technical revisions." The figure clearly shows that the policy changes, including those in the 1997 budget agreement, were not the source of the improved outlook. In fact, for FY 2000 and FY 2001, policy changes added slightly to the deficit.

FIGURE 10.2. ACCOUNTING FOR THE CHANGE IN THE CONGRESSIONAL BUDGET OFFICE'S SURPLUS PROJECTIONS BETWEEN JANUARY 1997 AND JULY 2000

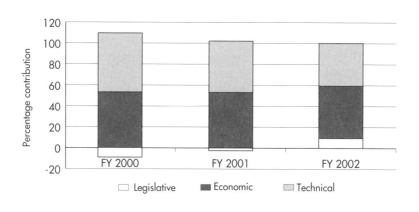

Source: Congressional Budget Office.

Roughly half of the budget surprise reflected improvements in the CBO's forecast for U.S. economic performance. For example:

- the estimated growth rate of potential output rose from roughly 2.1 percent to roughly 3.0 percent;

- the baseline level of potential GDP was revised up several times on the assumption that previous output surprises reflected permanent increases in potential output, and not just transitory influences;

- the assumed NAIRU was lowered from 5.8 percent in 1997 to 5.1 percent in July 2000; and

- the estimated share of taxable income in GDP was raised, due partly to an unanticipated reduction in (untaxed) benefits as a share of compensation.

In effect, many of the good luck factors that we discussed earlier were also responsible for the improved budget outlook.

The remaining half of the budget surprise is attributed to "technical changes"—mainly upward shifts in the functions relating tax collections to key economic variables. Why did the tax function relating revenues to GDP shift up so markedly? Subsequent analysis by the CBO using Internal Revenue Service data shows that several factors were at work. Taxable income rose faster than GDP because of strong capital gains, rising distributions from 401(k) plans, and the slow growth of untaxed benefits that we discussed earlier. The ratio of total taxes paid to adjusted gross income (AGI) also rose substantially—because of bracket creep and disproportionately strong income growth among high-income taxpayers, particularly in the forms of bonuses, stock options, and partnership income. For example, the share of AGI earned by those whose AGI exceeded $200,000 rose from 14.5 percent in 1993 to 20.6 percent in 1998, and their share of tax liabilities increased from 29.8 percent to 39.8 percent. The consequence of all this was an increase in the ratio of federal revenues to GDP of about 2.5 percentage points between 1994 and 2000—despite the 1997 tax cuts.[5] During the 2000 presidential campaign and after, this increase in effective tax rates would become a major political issue.

A final macroeconomic question relating to fiscal policy concerns the likely impact of the budget rules adopted in 1999 on future surpluses and trends in national saving. In the budget law passed in November 1999, Congress and the administration shifted the norm for fiscal policy fundamentally by declaring the Social Security surplus (then roughly $125 billion) off-budget and forever untouchable.[6] With surprisingly little fanfare or debate, the fiscal bar was thus raised enormously. When Bill Clinton took office in 1993, "balancing the budget" meant eliminating the deficit in the unified budget, including the Social Security surplus. The far more stringent goal of balancing the budget excluding Social Security was unthinkable. Now, however, "balancing the budget" means precisely that.[7]

With an off-budget surplus of $150 billion in fiscal year 2000, projected to rise to $331 billion by 2011, this "definitional" change actually implies a giant step toward boosting public saving.[8] If future Congresses succeed in avoiding on-budget deficits, the new fiscal benchmark will result in unified budget surpluses that range between 1.5 percent and 2 percent of GDP for over a decade—until the baby boomers begin to retire.[9]

However, the 1997–2001 budget surprise was so large that in January 2001, the CBO projected not only off-budget surpluses but also on-budget surpluses. Prior to the enactment of tax cut legislation this May, the on-budget surplus was projected to rise from $86 billion in 2000 to a mind-boggling $558 billion in 2011—$3.1 trillion in total over the next decade. How best to use these large on-budget surpluses became, of course, a central part of the political debate under the new rules of the fiscal game. Should they be used for tax cuts, for new spending initiatives, to shore up the finances of Social Security and Medicare, and/or to pay down more debt?[10] President George W. Bush made a big tax cut his top priority and succeeded in enacting a tax cut package that uses the lion's share (or more) of the surplus. He argued that the looming surpluses make it that much more affordable.

One cynical, but perhaps accurate, interpretation of the bipartisan agreement reached in 2000 to put the Social Security (and Medicare) surpluses in a tamper-proof "lock-box" might see it as the product of deadlock over competing policy priorities. Republicans favored tax cuts; Democrats were more inclined toward "new" spending; and, absent an agreement to do either, the surpluses were left to pile up and go to paying down the debt. Placing the surpluses in a lock-box had the further political advantage of making them unavailable to the opposing party in the event that it could muster a sufficient congressional majority. Perhaps most surprising of all, polls during the 2000 election campaign and after suggested that voters were attracted to the strategy of reducing the national debt—preferring it even over tax cuts.

Whatever its political motivation, the emergence of sizable budget surpluses in the decade before the baby boomers retire is probably desirable on long-run, public-finance grounds. These surpluses boost national saving and promote capital formation, which should help to sustain more rapid productivity growth. Using the surpluses to pay down the national debt also means that the interest burden in the federal budget will be substantially lower when the baby boomers retire, leaving more room in the budget for higher projected outlays on Social Security and Medicare. Already, economists and others are debating how financial markets will function without Treasury debt for benchmarking, how the Federal Reserve will conduct monetary policy once the debt is gone, and whether and how the federal government should acquire private assets.[11] We leave an analysis of these fascinating issues to the chroniclers of the next decade of macroeconomic history.

11.

CONCLUSIONS

LESSONS FOR POLICY

Readers with sufficient patience have now followed us through a long historical discourse—replete with much data and factual detail, plus a number of econometric model simulations. Our justification for telling the tale at such length is the importance of understanding this episode. It is, after all, one of the great shining moments of American economic history, and we would like to be able to replicate it. But how did we do it? And what lessons should policymakers carry away from the story? These are the questions we address in this chapter.

A BRIEF SUMMARY

First, a brief recapitulation of the story is in order, so we can see the proverbial forest amidst the numerous and leafy trees of earlier chapters.

The Fabulous Decade began around 1992 or 1993 under a set of propitious circumstances: the process of restoring fiscal probity was in train thanks to the 1990 budget agreement, monetary policy was pressing firmly on the gas pedal, many American industries had been profoundly restructured, and the economy was growing nicely. Fortunately, U.S. policymakers, led by Bill Clinton and Alan Greenspan, were wise enough to capitalize on this opportunity by continuing the fiscal consolidation and by maintaining extremely loose monetary policy until early 1994. Operating in tandem, this combination of promised fiscal tightening and loose money not only gave GDP a boost but also shifted its composition strongly toward investment.

Once the economy had built up enough forward momentum, the Federal Reserve expertly removed its foot from the accelerator and applied it to the brake—but lightly enough to achieve the proverbial soft landing in 1995. This successful bit of fine-tuning marked a departure from historical norms: most previous episodes of monetary tightening had ushered in recessions. While undoubtedly skillful, the Fed was also lucky that no major shock came along in 1994–95 to spoil its attempted soft landing. Folk wisdom holds that "I'd rather be lucky than good." The Fed was both.

Starting in 1995–96, the U.S. economy was blessed by a series of favorable supply shocks that no one could have anticipated. Foremost among these was the acceleration of productivity—the arrival of the much-heralded New Economy. By conventional definitions, labor productivity stems from two sources: technological advance and capital deepening. Both were in overdrive in the late 1990s. Part of the capital deepening can be attributed to the change in the policy mix—after all, higher investment was the basic goal of the tight budget/easy money mix. But the boom in information technology probably contributed much more to both total factor productivity growth and capital deepening (by lowering the cost of capital). It also undoubtedly helped power the soaring stock market—which rose to heights in 1999–2000 that proved to be unwarranted.

However, the technology spurt was not the only favorable supply shock. The costs of fringe benefits, especially health insurance, decelerated sharply in 1994 and 1995, moderating wage settlements and perhaps shifting the Phillips curve. The dollar soared from 1995 to 1998, driving down import prices. Oil prices declined steadily throughout 1997 and 1998. And, on top of all this good news, data revisions raised the real growth rate and reduced the measured inflation rate, making appearances even better than reality—which was good enough.

Favorable supply shocks like these allow a nation to enjoy some combination of lower inflation and faster real growth. Importantly, the Federal Reserve—whether by design or by accident—took a good deal of the largesse in the form of faster growth and lower unemployment. This it did mainly by forbearance, rather than by easing monetary policy. In fact, the FOMC held the funds rate virtually constant from January 1996 until September 1998.

Many of these positive developments—especially the faster growth and the booming stock market—also contributed to the remarkable turnaround in the federal budget position: from a unified deficit of $164 billion in fiscal 1995 to a surplus of $236 billion by fiscal 2000.

At this writing, the Fed is attempting to achieve the second soft landing in five years. If that can be accomplished, it would be truly remarkable. But the Fed is having its troubles. The stock market has tumbled, and economic growth in the first half of 2001 looks extremely weak.[1]

FIVE LESSONS FOR POLICYMAKERS

Perhaps the most obvious lesson from this period is that it is smart to be president of the United States or chairman of the Federal Reserve Board when large, favorable supply shocks come along. But that is not a very useful piece of advice. What other lessons can future policymakers glean from the Fabulous Decade? We would like to call attention, somewhat tentatively, to five.

Lesson 1 is the well-known point about the monetary-fiscal policy mix that we have made several times: *tight government budgets and (relatively) easy monetary policy can create a pro-investment macroeconomic climate by holding down real interest rates.* The resulting high rates of investment should then push up productivity and real wages. Economists have been preaching this gospel for decades. And it all seemed to work out according to Hoyle (actually, quite a bit better) in the United States in the 1990s, when the 1980s mix of tax cuts and tight money was finally and decisively reversed.

But did the policy mix really drive the investment boom of the 1990s? Our two macroeconometric models are doubtful. One major reason is a channel that textbook presentations often leave out: while lower interest rates stimulate investment spending, they also boost stock market values—which in turn spur consumption (via the wealth effect) more than investment.[2] Specifically, when we simulated the effects of tighter budgets—balanced by easier money to hold the time path of unemployment constant—most of the rise in government saving was cancelled out by lower personal saving, leaving the investment share of GDP up only slightly. The main impetus to investment, it appears, came from the surge in productivity.

The underlying reality, however, is probably messier than the models recognize. For example, while faster productivity growth undoubtedly spurs both more investment and faster GDP growth, just as the models say, a rapidly growing, high-investment economy probably also speeds up (embodied) technical progress. Why else did the explosion in information technology—which was, after all, a worldwide phenomenon—yield such rich productivity dividends in the United States, but not in Europe or Japan?

Lesson 2 is related: *what we normally think of as "contractionary" fiscal policy need not harm economic growth.* One reason is implicit in what we just said: expansionary monetary policy can offset any demand-reducing effects of budget cuts and tax hikes. But the 1993 budget agreement appears to have done more than that; it seems actually to have spurred the growth of aggregate demand even with no easing of monetary policy. The bond market, it appears, did the work for the Fed, as declining expected future deficits pulled down current long-term interest rates.

But "need not" is not synonymous with "will not." We argued earlier that a particularly fortuitous set of circumstances, market psychology, and design features of the budget agreement combined to ignite the 1993 bond market rally. We would not bet that this constellation can be replicated regularly, and hence we would not bet that all (nor even most) fiscal contractions will be expansionary.[3] Still, under the right circumstances, the trick can be pulled off. And it appears to have been done in 1993.

Lesson 3 is also one that we advance rather tentatively. In considering the experience of the 1990s, we are impressed by the fact that *well-designed fiscal policy rules can effectively constrain spending*—and apparently did so in the United States. The Budget Enforcement Act of 1990, with its spending caps and PAYGO procedures, is the most important example in this history. When it replaced the ill-conceived Gramm-Rudman-Hollings rules, things started to fall into place. But the recent decision to take Social Security "off budget," thereby redefining what it means to balance the budget, is another example that will, we believe, be important in years to come.[4] Nonetheless, it must be admitted that even well-designed rules can outlive their usefulness.

Having briefly extolled (good) rules, we hasten to add that the Fabulous Decade seems also to have resurrected an idea that most economists thought had died in the 1970s. Our *Lesson 4* is that it now appears that *fine-tuning is at least possible*. If not, we would like to know what Alan Greenspan has been up to since 1992. Indeed, we nominate Greenspan as the greatest fine-tuner in history. Once again, however, a caution is in order: to declare that something is possible is not to assert that it can be done easily or regularly. Successful fine-tuning requires a blend of skill and luck that may well be rare.[5] Alan Greenspan has had both, in abundance; others have had neither. And some people feel that even Greenspan's luck may have run out in the Fed's 1999–2000 tightening cycle, which went too far, according to some critics.

Furthermore, nothing in the history of the 1990s makes us at all optimistic about the feasibility of fiscal fine-tuning—the sort of thing that Walter Heller (1966) preached and tried to practice back in the 1960s. At least in the United States, the federal budget-making process looks extremely cumbersome, highly politicized, and not terribly responsive to economic logic. It is not for naught that Congress has shackled itself with rules. Among economists, there is an evolving tacit consensus that demand management should be left to monetary policy while fiscal policy is used as a long-run allocative tool—although the Bush administration fought this consensus by selling a large income tax cut on stabilization-policy grounds.[6] Without elevating this principle to the status of a commandment, for we must allow for exceptions, we agree that monetary, not fiscal, policy should carry most of the stabilization burden—at least in countries that have independent and capable central banks.

And that leads us to *Lesson 5: to achieve good macroeconomic outcomes, the central bank should have sensible objectives that include aversion to both inflation and unemployment.* During the Fabulous Decade, the Greenspan Fed revealed itself to be much enamored of economic growth—much more so than, say, the old Bundesbank or the current European Central Bank, with its mandate to pursue price stability only. It is true that the favorable supply shocks of the later 1990s cut the FOMC a lot of slack: even though they allowed aggregate demand to soar, inflation fell. But think about what the Fed did both before and after the good luck period (1996–98). By the fall of 1995, Greenspan had already been chairman of the Fed for eight years, and during that time the inflation rate had been beaten down from about 4 percent to about 3 percent. Does that suggest a single-minded devotion to the goal of price stability? And after core CPI inflation bottomed out at just below 2 percent at the end of 1999, it crept up more than 0.5 percentage point (as of this writing) without any noticeable effort by the Fed to push it back down.[7] Headline inflation has roughly doubled, largely because of rising energy prices, and the Fed has essentially swallowed this increase with barely a whimper.

The Federal Reserve's attitudes toward inflation and unemployment— and especially the way it "split" the gains offered by the supply shocks— go a long way, we believe, toward explaining why the Fabulous Decade was so fabulous.

NOTES

CHAPTER 1

1. Here, and throughout the book (except where noted), we use the latest revised data rather than the contemporaneous data that people were seeing at the time. According to contemporaneous data, the productivity trend was closer to 1 percent.

CHAPTER 2

1. Real average hourly earnings, as measured by the Department of Labor, *declined* almost 14 percent between 1973 and 1993. But those numbers were misleading for two main reasons: they overdeflated by using the "old" CPI, and they excluded fringe benefits, which grew faster than straight wages. During that same twenty-year period, real compensation per hour, which includes fringes and is deflated by the "new" CPI, *rose* 17 percent.

2. With the numbers in use at the time, output per hour in nonfarm business grew at a 1.3 percent average compound annual rate while real compensation advanced less than 0.6 percent per annum. With current numbers, these two figures are both higher—1.9 percent and 0.9 percent respectively—but the gap is even larger. Why such a large gap between productivity and compensation? One reason is that the prices of nonconsumer goods and services (for example, investment goods) rose less than consumer prices. This factor alone accounts for more than half the gap: nominal compensation deflated by the implicit deflator for nonfarm business product rose at 1.5 percent per annum. The rest was accounted for by rising markups.

3. Calculations made by the Economic Policy Institute show that median real wages (not total compensation, but properly deflated) fell by 5 percent between 1973 and 1993. At the twentieth percentile, they fell even more

(–9.4 percent); at the eightieth percentile, they rose (3.6 percent). See Lawrence Mishel, Jared Bernstein, and John Schmitt, *The State of Working America 2000–01*, (Ithaca, N.Y.: Cornell University Press, 2001), pp. 124, Table 2.6.

4. Eugene Carlson, "Campaign '92: While Voters Still Sing the Blues about the Economy, Hints of Optimism Emerge," *Wall Street Journal*, September 18, 1992, p. A6.

5. Jessica Lee and Bob Minzesheimer, "Statistics Do Support What Bush Is Saying," *USA Today*, October 27, 1992, p. 6A.

6. However, the productivity-enhancing effects of what was called "downsizing" were frequently exaggerated and may not have even existed. See, for example, Martin Baily, Eric Bartelsman, and John Haltiwanger, "Downsizing and Productivity Growth: Myth or Reality?" in D. G. Mayes, ed., *Sources of Productivity Growth in the 1980s* (Cambridge: Cambridge University Press, 1995).

7. The term is misleading because average establishment size did not fall in the late 1980s and early 1990s, except in manufacturing. Layoff announcements captured a great deal of public attention, but gross layoffs always greatly exceed net reductions in employment. However, there was plenty of labor-market churning during this period.

8. These numbers come from various issues of the AMA's annual publication, which has changed names several times over the years but is now called the *American Management Association Survey of Staffing and Structure*. The name changes are themselves revealing: in 1991, the report was called the *American Management Association Survey of Downsizing and Assistance to Displaced Workers*.

9. See Henry S. Farber, "Job Loss in the United States, 1981–1999," Working Paper #452, Industrial Relations Section, Princeton University, April 2001. While the sample is random, there are other drawbacks. First, the data come only in three-year increments, so it is hard to isolate timing. Second, a worker is considered "displaced" if the firm terminates her job but moves her to another job in the same company—which we would not consider to be job loss. Third, Farber's tabulations cover only people between ages 20 and 64.

CHAPTER 3

1. We are tacitly using the twelve-month moving average as an admittedly imperfect proxy for expected inflation. The real funds rate is, of course, not the only possible measure of monetary policy. It ignores, among other things, the exchange rate, the levels of longer-term interest rates, and equity prices—variables that are included in some broader indices of financial conditions.

2. For recent evidence in favor of this hypothesis, see Allen Berger, Margaret Kyle, and Joseph Scalise, "Did U.S. Bank Supervisors Get Tougher During the Credit Crunch? Did They Get Easier During the Banking Boom? Did It Matter to Bank Lending?" NBER Working Paper No. 7689, National Bureau of Economic Research, Cambridge, Mass., May 2000.

3. Federal Open Market Committee (hereinafter FOMC) meeting transcript, September 23, 1993, p. 36.

4. The acronym stands for Washington University Macro Model; it was originally developed by Laurence Meyer, now a Fed governor. We are extremely grateful to David Reifschneider of the Federal Reserve Board and his staff, and to Joel Prakken and Chris Varvares of Macroeconomic Advisers, for running simulations on their respective models for us.

5. Large econometric models are essentially very high-order difference equations. So seemingly subtle differences in specification can lead to very different dynamics.

6. The notation "1992:2" refers to the second quarter of 1992; this notation is used throughout the volume.

CHAPTER 4

1. See Bob Woodward, *The Agenda: Inside the Clinton White House* (New York: Simon and Schuster, 1994), especially Chapters 11 and 12.

2. Two major examples: a small "stimulus package" that Clinton had included as a kind of insurance policy against a relapse into recession was rejected by Congress, as was a proposed broad-based energy tax (the BTU tax).

3. FOMC meeting transcript, July 6–7, 1993, p. 66.

4. As noted earlier, some people would say this process began with Ross Perot.

5. However, critics did argue that raising the top income tax rate would not raise much revenue. See, for example, Martin Feldstein, "Clinton's Path to Wider Deficits," *Wall Street Journal*, February 23, 1993, p. A-20.

6. Cumulative economic growth over the 1992–98 period (which was relevant to the budget numbers) was about 1.4 percent less in the CBO's forecast than in the administration's forecast. See White House, *A Vision of Change for America*, February 17, 1993, Table 3-2, p. 25.

7. Note that the GDP gains in the WUMM model are given back in 1995 and 1996.

8. See Stephen J. Turnovsky and Marcus H. Miller, "The Effects of Government Expenditures on the Term Structure of Interest Rates," *Journal of Money, Credit and Banking* 16, no. 1 (February 1984): 16–33 and Olivier Blanchard, "Current and Anticipated Deficits, Interest Rates and

Economic Activity," *European Economic Review* 25 (May–June 1984): 7–27.

9. FOMC meeting transcript, March 23, 1993, p. 6.

10. FOMC meeting transcript, May 18, 1993, p. 28.

11. FOMC meeting transcript, February 2–3, 1993, p. 27.

12. FOMC meeting transcript, September 23, 1993, p. 5.

13. As reported by Bob Woodward, *Maestro: Greenspan's Fed and the American Boom* (New York: Simon and Schuster, 2000), p. 221.

CHAPTER 5

1. The real growth rate averaged 3.2 percent from 1991:4 to 1993:4.

2. Of the other four dissidents, two did not have a vote at that meeting and the other two voted along with the chairman after verbalizing their disagreements. This and other such information about FOMC meetings comes from the published transcripts.

3. Common estimates of the NAIRU then placed it around 6 percent. The Fed's staff estimate was a little higher. The actual unemployment rate in February 1994 was 6.6 percent.

4. Two positions on the Board of Governors were vacant at the time. They subsequently would be filled by the authors.

5. FOMC meeting transcript, February 3–4, 1994, p. 53.

6. FOMC meeting transcript, February 3–4, 1994, p. 55.

7. This idea was subsequently codified as the "opportunistic disinflation" strategy: prevent inflation from drifting higher and seize opportunities (such as favorable supply shocks or accidental recessions) to push inflation down. See Athanasios Orphanides and David Wilcox, "The Opportunistic Approach to Disinflation," Finance and Economics Discussion paper No. 24, Board of Governors of the Federal Reserve System, 1996.

8. We use the definition of neutrality suggested by Alan Blinder, *Central Banking in Theory and Practice* (Cambridge, Mass.: MIT Press, 1998): the funds rate that, once all the lags have worked themselves out, is consistent with neither rising nor falling inflation.

9. See statements by Governor Wayne Angell and chief monetary economist Donald Kohn in the FOMC meeting transcript, December 1993.

10. FOMC meeting transcript, March 1994, p. 44.

11. FOMC meeting transcript, July 1994, p. 15.

12. FOMC meeting transcript, September 1994, p. 39.

13. Antulio Bomfim, "The Equilibrium Federal Funds Rate and the Indicator Properties of Term-Structure Spreads," *Economic Inquiry* 35 (1997): 830–46.

14. A very long time period is needed to apply this method because there is no reason to think that shocks average to zero over short periods.

15. FOMC meeting transcript, January 31–February 1, 1995, p. 104.

16. With a lower growth rate of final sales, a lower level of inventory investment suffices to keep inventory/sales ratios at constant levels. This did indeed happen in 1995. After averaging about $67 billion (1996 chained) dollars in 1994, inventory investment declined to just $30 billion in 1995.

17. FOMC meeting transcript, January 31–February 1, 1995, p. 108.

18. On this, see Laurence Meyer, "Monetary Policy and the Bond Market: Complements or Substitutes?" speech before the Fixed Income Summit of PSA, The Bond Market Trade Association, Washington, D.C., September 12, 1997.

19. Alan Greenspan, testimony before the Committee on Banking, Housing, and Urban Affairs, February 22, 1995.

20. See, for example, FOMC minutes, February 1996.

21. The (current) data reported here have seen substantial revision since 1996. GDP data available at the end of 1996 recorded real GDP growth of just 2.0 percent in the second half of 1995.

22. The first alternative assumes in addition that long-term bond yields spike sharply following the beginning of Fed tightening in 1995:3 (see Table 5.1), analogous to their actual behavior in 1994 following the Fed's shift to tighter policy.

CHAPTER 6

1. The cyclical low of the unemployment rate, 3.9 percent, was reached in September and October of 2000.

2. In 2000, the FOMC adopted this index for its official inflation forecasts. As the table shows, inflation since 1993 is substantially lower when gauged by the PCE instead of the CPI-U. The average gap is about 0.6 percentage point. The two series differ mainly in their treatment of medical care and housing.

3. For example, profit margins were widening despite allegedly intense competitive pressures and rising wages.

4. Equations (1), (2), and (3) generate a long-run Phillips curve which is vertical at the NAIRU, $U = U^*$. Some argue, however, that the long-run Phillips curve is probably not vertical at low inflation rates, due to the reluctance of workers to accept nominal wage cuts and/or their failure to incorporate inflation expectations into wage bargains on a point-for-point basis. See George A. Akerlof, William T. Dickens and George L. Perry, "The Macroeconomics of Low Inflation," *Brookings Papers on Economic Activity* 1:1996, 1–76; and George A. Akerlof, William T. Dickens, and George L. Perry, "Near-Rational Wage and Price Setting and the Long-Run Phillips

Curve," *Brookings Papers on Economic Activity* 1:2000, 1–60. This criticism notwithstanding, (1) – (3) suffice as a simplified organizational framework for our discussion of supply shocks.

5. A similar graph using the PCE measure of inflation (not shown) looks substantially identical.

6. Alas, this excellent fit would not last long, as we discuss below.

7. In efficiency wage models, any shock that leads workers to view their outside opportunities less favorably will lower equilibrium unemployment, U^*, reduce the efficiency wage premium, and raise firms' markups. An unusually low level of quits (into unemployment), given the duration of unemployment, suggested an increase in job insecurity.

8. See Alan Greenspan, Testimony before the Committee on Banking, Housing and Urban Affairs, February 22, 1995, p. 5; and Testimony before the Committee on Banking, Housing, and Urban Affairs, February 20, 1996, p. 9.

9. On this and several other matters discussed in this paragraph, see Stephanie Schmidt and Christopher Thompson, "Have Workers' Beliefs about Job Security Been Keeping Wage Inflation Low? Evidence from Public Opinion Data," Milken Institute Working Paper 97-4, October 1997, and Stephanie Schmidt, "Long-Run Trends in Workers' Beliefs about Their Own Job Security: Evidence from the General Social Survey," *Journal of Labor Economics* 17 (October 1999): S127–S141.

10. On job loss, see Henry S. Farber, "Job Loss in the United States, 1981–1999," Working Paper #452, Industrial Relations Section, Princeton University, April 2001.

11. The percentage of estimated working time lost due to work stoppages involving one thousand or more workers hit a postwar low of 0.01 in 1992 and remained at or below 0.02 through 1999. See U.S. Department of Labor, Bureau of Labor Statistics, "Work Stoppages Summary," February 9, 2001.

12. See, for example, Alan Krueger and Helen Levy, "Accounting for the Slowdown in Employer Health Care Costs," 1996 Proceedings of the 89th Annual Conference on Taxation, National Tax Association, Tax Institute of America, Washington, D.C., 1997.

13. These three benefits comprise about 96 percent of what is called "other labor income" (supplements to wages and salaries other than employer contributions to social insurance).

14. For evidence, see Lawrence Summers, "Some Simple Economics of Mandated Benefits," *American Economic Review*, 79(2), May 1989, 177–83; Jonathan Gruber, "The Incidence of Payroll Taxation: Evidence from Chile," *Journal of Labor Economics* 15 (3, Part 2) July 1997, S72–S101; and Jonathan Gruber and Alan Krueger, "The Incidence of Mandated Employer Provided Insurance: Lessons from Workers' Compensation Insurance," David Bradford, ed., *Tax Policy and the Economy* (Cambridge, Mass.: MIT

Press, 1991), 111–43. Gruber and Krueger found that changes in employers' costs for workers' compensation are largely shifted to workers in the form of lower wages.

15. A price-price Phillips curve augmented to include the markup of price over trend unit labor costs is stable and fits the data well throughout the 1990s, whereas standard specifications show evidence of a substantial NAIRU shift beginning in 1994:4. See Flint Brayton, John Roberts, and John Williams, "What's Happened to the Phillips Curve?" Federal Reserve Board discussion paper, September 1999. According to their estimates, the markup swelled between 1993 and 1995 and declined to its mean between 1996 and 1998, holding down inflation during the later period.

16. We simulate the benefit shock by adjusting each model's counterpart of equation (1). The direct impact of the benefit shock on compensation growth in the simulations averages –1.0 percent, –0.7 percent, and –1.1 percent in 1995, 1996, and 1997 respectively, and –0.1 percent in 1998 and 1999.

17. The simulations reported in Table 6.1 ignore any direct impact of slower medical care inflation on consumer price inflation. WUMM simulations that also include a direct impact of slower escalation of medical prices in the PCE price index produce CPI inflation rates that are 0.1–0.2 percent lower than those reported in Table 6.1.

18. Princeton economist Henry Farber found that, conditioning on the unemployment rate, permanent layoffs were unusually high between 1993 and 1997. Permanent layoffs subsequently declined to more normal levels. See Henry Farber, "Has the Rate of Job Loss Increased in the Nineties?" Working Paper #394, Industrial Relations Section, Princeton University, January 1998.

19. Our simulation holds the Federal Reserve Board's broad (thirty-five-country) price-level adjusted exchange rate at its 1995:2 level.

20. In the WUMM model, we held the refiners' acquisition cost of imported oil at its 1996:1 level of $18.38 per barrel. In the FRB-US model, we held the unit value oil import price at its 1996:1 level of $17.46 per barrel.

21. A convenient table of these changes can be found in *Economic Report of the President*, February 1999, page 94. For more details, see Kenneth J. Stewart and Stephen B. Reed, "CPI Research Series Using Current Methods, 1978–98," *Monthly Labor Review*, June 1999 and *Economic Report of the President*, February 2000, p. 61.

22. Between 1992 and 1994, a period in which no significant methodological changes were implemented, the CPI-U rose 0.39 percent more rapidly, on average, than the CPI-U-RS. The introduction of a new market basket with revised expenditure weights in 1998 lowered inflation rates in both series by an estimated further 0.17 percent per annum. Thus, methodological changes likely lowered inflation in the CPI-U by about 0.6 percent per annum between 1995 and 1999.

23. See Michael J. Boskin et al., *Toward a More Accurate Measure of the Cost of Living*, Final Report to the Senate Finance Committee from the Advisory Commission to Study the Consumer Price Index, December 4, 1996, Appendix Figures A1, A2.

24. The CPI revisions also reduced the inflation measures in the national income and product accounts (GDP deflator, PCE deflator, and so on), though by smaller amounts. But these measures garner much less public attention.

25. Laurence Meyer, Remarks at the National Association for Business Economics 40th Anniversary Annual Meeting, Washington, D.C., October 5, 1998.

26. Laurence Meyer, Remarks at the Charlotte Economics Club, Charlotte, NC, January 16, 1997; and "Structural Change and Monetary Policy," Remarks at Federal Reserve Bank of San Francisco, March 3, 2000.

27. Models explaining the falling saving rate by the rising stock market are quite successful during this period—and beyond.

28. Alan Greenspan, "The Challenge of Central Banking in a Democratic Society," Francis Boyer Lecture of The American Enterprise Institute for Public Policy Research, December 5, 1996.

29. See FOMC minutes, September 1997.

30. This was the time, for example, that a stunning gap opened up between the yields on thirty-year and twenty-nine-year Treasury bonds.

CHAPTER 7

1. The growth in nominal compensation, as measured by the employment cost index, accelerated only slightly between 1995 and 1999, rising, on a fourth-quarter over fourth-quarter basis, from 2.7 percent in 1995 to 3.4 percent in 1999. During the first three quarters of 2000, however, ECI compensation rose at a 4.5 percent annual pace. A second measure of compensation in the nonfarm business sector shows greater overall acceleration through 1999. This alternative measure of compensation rose 2.6 percent in 1995 and 4.7 percent in 1999. This measure of compensation growth, however, declined from mid 1998 through the first quarter of 2000.

CHAPTER 8

1. It has long been known that productivity tends to rise when output grows rapidly.

2. See Robert M. Solow, *New York Times Book Review*, July 12, 1987, p. 36.

3. Named for Intel's Gordon Moore, Moore's Law predicted that the number of transistors integrated on circuits would double every eighteen months.

4. Stephen Oliner and Daniel Sichel, "The Resurgence of Growth in the Late 1990s: Is Information Technology the Story?" Board of Governors of the Federal Reserve, Washington, D.C., March 2000.

5. Robert J. Gordon, "Does the 'New Economy' Measure up to the Great Inventions of the Past?" *Journal of Economic Perspectives* 14, no. 4 (Fall 2000): 49–74.

6. According to the basic theory of investment, it is important to distinguish between the effects of *lower* prices versus *falling* prices on the cost of capital, and hence on investment. A lower price of capital goods spurs investment spending. But a more rapid pace of (expected) price decline deters spending because it represents (expected) capital losses. In practice, the price-level effect was the dominant one.

7. Oliner and Sichel, ibid.

8. See Laurence Ball and Robert Moffitt, "Productivity Growth and the Phillips Curve," paper prepared for The Century Foundation-Russell Sage Foundation conference on sustainable employment, January 2001.

9. U.S. Phillips curve equations that include a productivity growth term typically find a significant (temporary) adverse impact of slower productivity growth on inflation. See Steven N. Braun, "Productivity and the NIIRU (and Other Phillips' Curve Issues)," Working Paper #34, Federal Reserve Board, Economic Activity Section, 1984, and Steven N. Braun and Ron Chen, "The NAIRU as a Policy Target: Refinements, Problems and Challenges," unpublished manuscript, 1996. See also *Economic Report of the President*, February 2000, pp. 90–91.

10. The simulation assumes that, after 1993, trend labor productivity in the nonfarm business sector continued to grow at its 1974–93 average of about 1.5 percent per year, rather than accelerating sharply. The assumed deviation of the level and growth rates of nonfarm business trend productivity from baseline are shown in the last two rows of Table 8.2.

11. In FRB-US model simulations that adjust the real federal funds rate to hold unemployment at baseline levels, the identical productivity shock lowers inflation by 0.7 percent relative to baseline in 1999.

12. In the WUMM model, this relative price is measured by the ratio of the PDE-computer price index to an index of nonfarm prices.

13. An alternative way to summarize the effect of the productivity shock on the Phillips curve tradeoff is in terms of its impact on the model's short-run NAIRU, which falls by about 0.4 percentage points in the FRB-US model and about 0.8 percentage points in the WUMM model during the second half of the 1990s.

CHAPTER 9

1. The personal saving rate declined from 8.7 percent in 1992 to 2.2 percent in 1999 (and then turned slightly negative).

2. For an extreme example, see James Glassman and Kevin Hassett, *Dow 36,000* (New York: Times Books), 1999, in which the authors essentially argue for a zero risk premium for equities. Less extreme versions simply hold that the equity premium fell.

CHAPTER 10

1. On a standardized basis—that is, adjusting for cyclical effects and for extraneous factors such as asset sales and meaningless shifts in the timing of receipts between one fiscal year and the next—the deficit as a share of potential GDP fell by 1.8 percentage points between 1992 and 1996. See Congressional Budget Office, *The Budget and Economic Outlook: Fiscal Years 2002–2011*, January 2001, Table F-3, p. 141.

2. One reason the 1997 agreement contained so little fiscal restraint is that the CBO announced at the last minute that it had underestimated future federal tax receipts by $45 billion per year between 1998 and 2002. (See Clay Chandler, "CBO Gives Negotiators a Windfall of $225 Billion in Tax Revenue," *Washington Post*, May 3, 1997, p. A15.) This eleventh-hour news led the budget negotiators to scrap some of the most painful cuts contained in their draft agreement. (See "Ducking the Hard Ones," *Washington Post*, May 6, 1997, p. A18.)

3. See White House, *Mid-session Review*, Fiscal Year 2000, June 1999.

4. The data underlying Figures 10.1 and 10.2 come from various issues of the series of publications by the CBO entitled *The Budget and Economic Outlook*. For each date, we chose CBO surplus projections that assume (counterfactually, as it later turned out) adherence to the discretionary spending caps in the 1997 Budget Agreement.

5. See Congressional Budget Office, *The Budget and Economic Outlook: Fiscal Years 2001–2010*, January 2000, pp. 52–58.

6. In addition to Social Security, the off-budget surplus also includes revenues and spending of the Postal Service. At this writing, there is some debate over whether President George W. Bush's budget request (including his large tax cuts) can be accommodated without "invading" the Social Security surplus.

7. In its mid-session review of the budget in 2000, the Clinton administration proposed placing the surpluses of Medicare's Hospital Insurance Fund off budget as well. (At present, Medicare is "on budget.") Then-

candidate Al Gore and both parties in Congress rushed to embrace this proposal. But then-candidate George W. Bush did not.

8. See Congressional Budget Office, *The Budget and Economic Outlook: Fiscal Years 2002–2011,* January 2001, Table 1-1, p. 2. These estimates assume that discretionary spending grows at the rate of inflation.

9. A sufficiently large recession could cause current on-budget surpluses to shrink or turn to deficits. In this event, Congress might decide to abandon the new budget rule.

10. Under the CBO's capped baseline, any proposal to raise appropriations above the 1997 caps is treated as "new spending," even if does no more than keep discretionary spending from declining in real terms.

11. On the first two issues, see, for example, Vincent Reinhart and Brian Sack, "The Economic Consequences of Disappearing Government Debt," *Brookings Papers on Economic Activity* 2 (2000): 163–209. On the last, Alan Greenspan created a stir in January 2001 when he opined that the federal government should not acquire private assets. A tax cut would be better, he said.

CHAPTER 11

1. At this printing (the numbers will subsequently be revised), the annualized growth rate of real GDP has averaged just 1.5 percent over the last two quarters of 2000 and the first quarter of 2001.

2. This is only partially offset by the fact that higher stock prices lower the cost of capital to firms.

3. As Robert Solow reminds us, those who promote the idea that, say, cutting government spending can be expansionary never suggest raising government spending to calm an overheating economy.

4. A recent paper argues that the new political economy rule will substantially change the impact of entitlement reforms and other budget policies on national saving. See Douglas Elmendorf and Jeffrey Liebman, "Social Security Reform and National Saving in an Era of Budget Surpluses," *Brookings Papers on Economic Activity* 2 (2000).

5. We would also argue, perhaps controversially, that greater transparency helps make fine tuning work. Since 1996, the markets have developed a better and better understanding of what the Fed was up to. In consequence, it was often said that long-term interest rates were "doing the Fed's work for it."

6. This is slightly odd, since the Bush tax proposal long predated the economic slowdown and was not designed to alleviate it. For example, the amount of tax cutting originally proposed for fiscal years 2001 and 2002 is small.

7. The Fed has been pretty clear that the 1999–2000 tightening cycle was intended to slow the growth rate of aggregate demand to that of aggregate supply, thereby capping inflation—not bringing inflation back to 2 percent.

INDEX

Note: Page numbers followed by letters *f, n,* and *t* refer to figures, notes, and tables, respectively.

ABOUT THE AUTHORS

ALAN S. BLINDER is the Gordon S. Rentschler Memorial Professor of Economics at Princeton University, a partner in the Promontory Financial Group, and vice chairman of The G7 Group. He was a member of President Clinton's original Council of Economic Advisers and then became vice chairman of the Federal Reserve Board—a post he held from 1994 until early 1996.

JANET L. YELLEN is the Eugene E. and Catherine M. Trefethen Professor of Business and professor of economics at the University of California at Berkeley. She served as a governor of the Federal Reserve (1994–97) and then as chair of the Council of Economic Advisers (1997–99).